Above: Looking out towards Ramsey Island
Front cover: St Brides's Haven
Back cover: Carew Castle

Written by: Trevor Barrett.

Revised and updated by: Miles Cowsill & Andrew Rogers.

Photography: Miles Cowsill and Chris Warren.

First published by Lily Publications 1992

First Premier Guide edition published 1995

This (9th) edition 2000

Copyright © 2000 Lily Publications. All rights reserved. Any reproduction in whole or in part is strictly prohibited. The content contained herein is based on the best available information at the time of research. The publishers assume no liability whatsoever arising from the publishing of material contained herein.

All accommodation advertised in this guide participates in the Wales Tourist Board's inspection scheme. If readers have any concern about the standards of any accommodation, please take the matter up directly with the provider of the accommodation, as soon as possible. Failing satisfaction, please contact the Wales Tourist Board, Development Services Unit, Brunel House, 2 Fitzalan Road, Cardiff CF2 1UY.

Published by Lily Publications, PO Box 9, Narberth, Pembrokeshire, Wales SA68 0YT.
Tel: +44 (0)1834) 891461, Fax:+44 (0)1834) 891463.   ISBN 1 899602 41 0.

Contents

Maps

medieval times and which still bears the remains of many 5th-century monastic huts. The cliffs backing the beach also boast an unusual feature - the Three Chimneys. These are horizontal beds of Silurian rock, more than 400 million years old, pushed up vertically by incredibly powerful earth movements. Parking for the beach is half a mile away in the large National Trust car park, and the nearest amenities are at the village of Marloes, about a mile from the beach. In 1999 Marloes Sands won a Seaside Award.

Martin's Haven: A small north-facing cove with a pebble beach. Boat trips operate from here to the Skomer Nature Reserve and facilities include toilets and parking. In 1999 Martin's Haven won a Seaside Award.

Musselwick Sands: This fine sandy beach, exposed only at low tide, is actually closer to the village of Marloes than is Marloes Sands. The cliffs are unstable and dangerous, and beware of being cut off by

Broad Haven

the incoming tide. Access is also difficult, along a steep path and over rocks. But the rewards are rare tranquillity and stunning views towards the St. David's Peninsula. There is limited parking at the start of the half-mile footpath to the beach, but no amenities.

St. Bride's Haven: This is a sheltered cove with a beach of shingle, pebbles and rock pools, enhanced by sand at low tide. The beach faces northwest, giving good views across St. Bride's Bay, and is protected from southwesterly winds. Interesting features near the beach include an early Christian cemetery with stone-lined graves, and the remains of an old limekiln. There is limited parking near the church. In 1999 St. Bride's Haven won a Seaside Award.

Little Haven: Little Haven is a small but attractive sandy cove tucked into the sheltered southeast corner of St. Bride's Bay. At low water you can walk the short distance along the shoreline to the otherwise inaccessible neighbouring beach known as The Settlands, and then on to Broad Haven - but always beware of being cut off by an incoming tide! Little Haven beach has a slipway for launching boats, including the lifeboat, so it must be kept clear. There is a pay-and-display car park in the village, close to the beach.

Broad Haven (west): A large and beautiful expanse of sand which at low water really lives up to its name, Broad Haven (not to be confused with the beach of the same name on the south coast) is very popular and within easy reach of Haverfordwest. It is a favourite with bathers and watersports enthusiasts, and also has a great deal to interest geologists - stacks, arches, intense folding and shattering of the cliffs, and a huge rock

15

Newgale

known as the Sleek Stone. The beach runs the entire length of Broad Haven village where the good facilities, including a choice of car parks, ensure that this is a busy and enjoyable holiday centre. In 1999 Broad Haven won a Seaside Award.

Druidston Haven: Enclosed on three sides by steep cliffs, this is a long sandy beach backed by a pebble bank. The cliffs at the southern end reveal traces of coal seams which overlay limestone and old red sandstone - old workings can even be seen. But beware of the incoming tide, which rises rapidly at this end of the beach. Bathers should also beware of strong currents. Access to the beach is by either of two footpaths, but parking (on the roadside) is very limited. The beach has no amenities.

Nolton Haven: This is a small sheltered beach of sand and shingle, with cliffs on either side. Coal mining once thrived at nearby Trefrane Colliery, and coal was shipped from here. Bathing at Nolton Haven has its dangers. At low water the currents can be unpredictable and if the red flag is flying it means that swimming is unsafe. There is a National Park car park above the beach.

Newgale Sands: West-facing Newgale is a broad expanse of flat sand wide open to Atlantic gales and stormy seas. While this means that in exceptionally bad conditions the sea can breach the high pebble bank and flood the road, in fairer weather Newgale is an idyllic spot for surfers and other water-sports enthusiasts. During summer months the beach is patrolled by lifeguards, who designate safe areas for swimmers, away from unpredictable currents and undertows. This superb beach, nearly two miles long at low tide, is also popular with sea anglers and walkers. At exceptionally low water, particularly spring tides, the preserved stumps and roots of ancient trees can be seen - the remnants of a prehistoric forest drowned when melting ice caused sea levels to rise dramatically at the end of the last Ice Age. Newgale also marks the western end of the Landsker Line. Parking facilities for the beach are good and in 1999 Newgale Sands won both a Seaside Award and a European Blue Flag.

North Coast

beach, but there are no amenities. In 1999 Caerfai Bay won a Seaside Award.

Caerbwdi Bay: This is a small sheltered beach of rock and pebble, with sand exposed at low tide. South facing, it is close to St. David's and is accessible via a half-mile footpath from the A487 Solva to St. David's road, where there is limited parking. The beach is popular with walkers but has no amenities.

Caerfai Bay: This is the nearest beach to St. David's and is popular with bathers, although at high tide the sand is completely covered, leaving only rocks and boulders. Unstable cliffs that should be avoided enclose the bay, south facing and well sheltered, but there are caves and rock pools to explore. A feature of the cliffs is the unusual purple sandstone, which was used in the building of St. David's Cathedral. Parking is available above the

Porthselau: This small sandy beach has rocky outcrops and gives superb views across Whitesands Bay to St. David' s Head. At very low tide it is possible to walk along the shoreline to the neighbouring beach at Whitesands, the coast path providing an escape route should you be cut off by the tide. There is limited parking along the track which leads to the beach from the St. David' s to St. Justinian road. The beach has no amenities.

Whitesands: Consistently rated one of Wales' very best seaside resorts, Whitesands is a large sandy beach in a magnificent setting, well known for its views and glorious sunsets. It is understandably popular, with safe swimming and surfing areas designated by the lifeguards who patrol here between

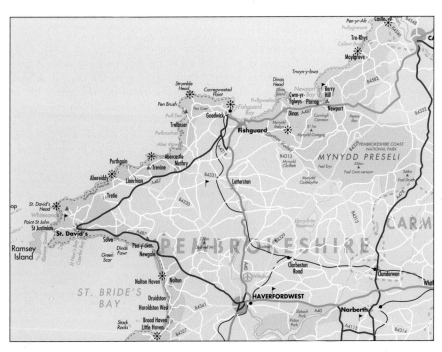

Whitesands

mid-June and early September. As at
nearby Newgale Sands, the remains of an
ancient drowned forest can sometimes be
seen at low tide. Away from the beach, this
is excellent walking country; a climb to the
summit of Carn Llidi, for example, reveals
stunning views over the St. David's
Peninsula, nearby Ramsey Island and
much of Pembrokeshire. St. David's with
its many attractions is also close by.
Facilities at the beach are good, including a
large car park. In 1999 Whitesands won
both the European Blue Flag Award and a
Seaside Award.

Porthmelgan: Just to the northwest of
Whitesands, near St. David's Head, is the
sandy and secluded beach of Porthmelgan.
Low tide reveals rock pools and caves, and
there are good seaward views of Ramsey

Island and the hazardous rocky reefs
known as the Bishops and Clerks. Access
to Porthmelgan is via the coast path from
St. David's Head or the car park at
Whitesands. The beach has no amenities.

Abereiddy Bay: A fascinating beach for
several reasons, not least its black sand -
the result of the waves constantly pounding
the slate cliffs. Also to be found here are
tiny fossil graptolites, present in shale
fragments, which are of geological
importance and should not be removed
from the beach. Just to the north of the
beach is the beautiful Blue Lagoon - a
flooded slate quarry that is as deep as the
cliffs are tall. Slate was quarried at
Abereiddy until 1904, and a narrow-gauge
railway ran to nearby Porthgain harbour,
from where the slate was shipped to ports

18

Abereiddy Bay

Pwllgwaelod

all round Britain. If bathing at Abereiddy, beware of undercurrents and undertows. Close to the beach is a large parking area, and in 1999 Abereiddy won a Seaside Award.

Traeth Llyfn: A beautiful sandy beach just a half-mile walk from Abereiddy. The National Trust owned Traeth Llyfn is enclosed by cliffs and headlands and has lots of rock pools. This is a dangerous beach for swimming, especially in rough seas, because of strong undertow. You should also be aware that the southern end of the beach is sometimes cut off before high tide. Access to the beach is down steep steps and there are no amenities here.

Trevine: A small shingle-and-sand beach enclosed by rugged cliffs, Trevine is not a bathing beach because of the rocks and unstable nature of the cliffs, but there are superb walks and views along the coast path in both directions. Access to the beach is via a short path, with limited roadside parking. The beach has no amenities, but in nearby Trevine village there are shops, toilets and other facilities.

Abercastle: This attractive cove, once a busy slate port, faces northwest and is a natural sheltered harbour. The small beach

is of muddy wet sand and shingle, and is much favoured by fishermen, boat enthusiasts, divers and walkers. Just west of the beach is Carreg Samson - a 4,500-year-old burial chamber. There is limited parking above the beach.

Abermawr: Another of Pembrokeshire's beaches to reveal the remains of a drowned forest at very low tides, Abermawr is a large sheltered bay with woods near the shoreline. A high pebble bank backs the beach and bathing can be dangerous in places because of currents. Access to the beach is via a short path from the roadside where there is limited parking. The beach has no amenities.

Pwllgwaelod: Nestling between the neck and shoulder of the Dinas Island promontory, on the western side, Pwllgwaelod is a small but attractive sandy beach with views towards Fishguard Bay and harbour. This is good cliff-walking territory. Nearby are Dinas Head, a nature trail and the beach at Cwm-yr-Eglwys.

Cwm-yr-Eglwys: Like Pwllgwaelod, this small shingle-and-pebble beach lies in a corner created by the Dinas Island promontory, but on the eastern side. It is a popular family beach, enhanced by sand at

19

low tide, with views across Newport Bay. It is also of historical interest; the scant remains of 12th-century St. Brynach's Church are evidence of the ferocious storm of October 1859 which not only destroyed the church but also wrecked over 100 ships off the western coast and, amongst other things, formed the huge pebble bank which still backs Newgale Sands. Parking for the beach is limited, in a private car park. In 1999 Cwm-yr-Eglwys won a Seaside Award.

Cwm-yr-Eglwys

Newport Parrog: The historic town of Newport stands near the mouth of the River Nevern, where there are two beaches - one on each side of the estuary. The Parrog is on the southern side, and although this is the more sheltered beach unpredictable currents make bathing dangerous. The area is rich in prehistoric sites, including Pentre Ifan burial chamber. In the car park above the beach you can pick up useful information from the Wales Wildlife Trust's caravan.

Newport Sands: By far the more popular of Newport's two beaches, this vast expanse of sand on the northern side of the Nevern estuary is backed by dunes and a golf course. This is a favourite spot for beach games, swimming, windsurfing, boating and other water-sports, but you should beware of dangerous currents around the mouth of the river. There is a large car park above the beach and limited parking on the sand. In 1999 Newport won a Seaside Award.

Ceibwr Bay: This beach, composed of pebbles and rock, is an ideal base for coastal walks, as the area boasts the highest cliffs in Pembrokeshire. The spectacular coastal scenery includes the Witches' Cauldron - a cave, blowhole and natural arch - and incredible folding of the cliff rock strata. Another attraction not to be missed is the sight of Atlantic grey seals swimming offshore or basking on rocks. Great care should be taken along the cliffs, particularly with children. Access to Ceibwr Bay is via a very narrow road from the village of Moylegrove, with limited roadside parking above the bay.

Poppit Sands: Poppit Sands is a large expanse of fine sand at the mouth of the Teifi estuary, and marks the northern border of Pembrokeshire and the northern end of the Pembrokeshire Coastal Path. Across the estuary is Cardiganshire, with the town of Cardigan itself just a couple of miles inland on the banks of the River Teifi. The proximity of the town has made Poppit Sands a very popular beach. It is sheltered from prevailing southwesterly winds, but beware of dangerous currents and take heed of the warning signs and lifeguard flags. The beach is backed by sand dunes and mudflats, both of which are sensitive, fragile environments important to wildlife, so please avoid them. There are good facilities near the beach, including a large car park. In 1999 Poppit Sands won a Seaside Award from the Tidy Britain Group.

Safety on the beach

Know where your children are at all times. Keep an eye on them, especially when they're swimming or playing at the water's edge. Children can drown even in very shallow water.

Make sure you always know where everyone else is. Let each other know if anyone is going swimming or leaving the beach for any reason.

Beware of being trapped by the tide coming in. You can find out about local currents and tides by ringing the coastguard - particularly important if you're going to a remote beach.

Don't play on rocks. And take care on groynes and breakwaters, noting where they are before you start swimming.

Never climb on cliffs and keep away from cliff edges. Even gentle slopes can be dangerous when they are wet.

Watch out for big waves coming in. They can sweep you off your feet even if you think you are standing somewhere safe.

Always take advice given by lifeguards, flags & notices.

SAFETY IN THE WATER
* **NEVER SWIM**
if there is a red flag flying
if you feel unwell
for at least an hour after a meal
when you are cold or tired
if you have been drinking alcohol.
* If you can, swim where there is a lifeguard on patrol, and always swim where there are other people.
* Always swim close to the beach and never out to sea.
* Don't stay in the water too long. You will get cold and tired.
* Don't use inflatable airbeds in the water. They can get blown out to sea.

* If you have a belly board, stay with the board and don't go out too far.
* Only use a snorkel if you are a good swimmer and the water is calm. Don't snorkel if you have breathing problems.
* Even a calm sea can be dangerous. Always take great care.
IF YOU SEE SOMEONE IN TROUBLE IN THE WATER
tell the lifeguard, or dial 999 and ask for the coastguard.

FLAGS YOU SHOULD KNOW

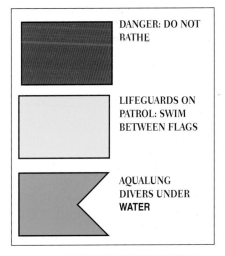

DANGER: DO NOT BATHE

LIFEGUARDS ON PATROL: SWIM BETWEEN FLAGS

AQUALUNG DIVERS UNDER WATER

TIDE AND WEATHER INFORMATION

For information on tides, see the local press (Western Telegraph, Tenby Observer and West Wales Guardian) or ring Milford Haven Coastguard on 01646 690909.

Weather forecasts are given regularly by BBC Radio 4, BBC Radio Wales, Radio Cymru and Swansea Sound. Radio 4's main weather forecasts are broadcast daily at 06.03, 06.55, 07.55, 08.58, 12.55, 17.55, 21.59 and 00.20.

Shipping forecasts are broadcast daily by Radio 4 at 05.55, 13.55, 17.50 and 00.33. Limited shipping forecasts are also given by Radio Wales, Radio Cymru and Swansea Sound.

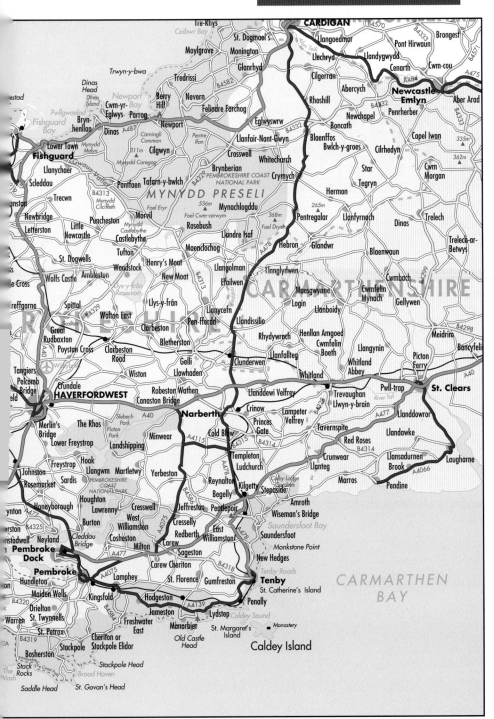

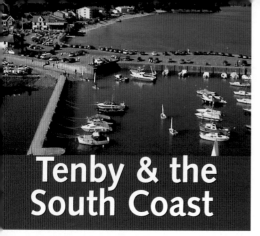

Tenby & the South Coast

South Pembrokeshire is often referred to as 'Little England beyond Wales' - a description which is a consequence of the Norman Conquest, since it was the Normans who effectively created a linguistic and cultural divide between the north and south of the county after they arrived in Pembrokeshire in 1093.

Today, this divide is still evident. South Pembrokeshire is indeed much more English than it is Welsh, and in North Pembrokeshire the reverse is true. But to visitors the differences are largely academic, if anything adding to the fascination and variety of this unspoilt corner of Wales' wonderful West Coast.

South Pembrokeshire has four main holiday centres - Tenby, Saundersfoot, Pembroke and Narberth. Tenby and its near neighbour Saundersfoot are among Britain's favourite seaside resorts, while the ancient town of Pembroke, which celebrated 900 years of history in 1993, boasts one of Britain' s best-preserved medieval castles. Narberth too is an historic town with a Norman castle, and it stands at the heart of a beautiful and tranquil area known as the Landsker Borderlands. All four centres are close to many visitor attractions and places of interest, and each provide an ideal base for wider exploration of the glorious South Pembrokeshire coastline and countryside.

Tenby harbour

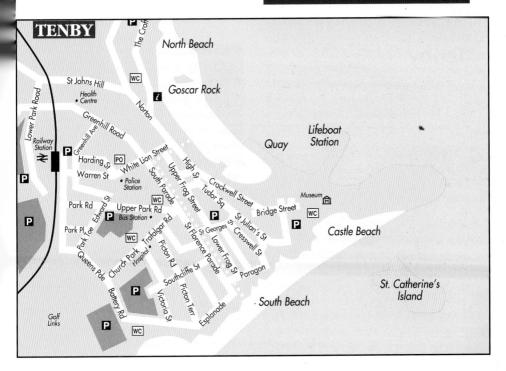

TENBY

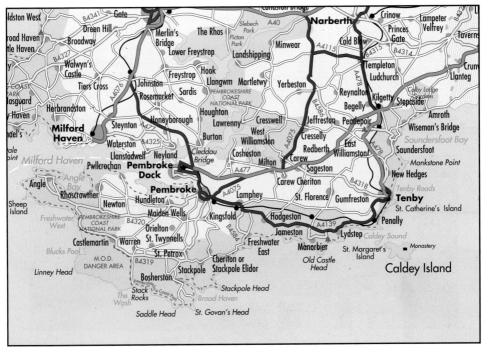

Tenby

Distances: Fishguard 36, Haverfordwest 19, Milford Haven 19, Narberth 10, Pembroke 10, St. David's 35, Saundersfoot 3, Carmarthen 27 and London 247.

Tenby's popularity as a resort goes back to the 18th century when the rich came here for the good of their health. A much wider circle of visitors began to arrive with the coming of the railway in 1866, but inevitably it was the wealthy Victorians who provided the finance that developed Tenby into one of Wales' most frequented holiday destinations.

Were those early visitors to return today, they would no doubt be surprised to discover that Tenby has changed very little since their time - certainly when compared with the way in which many other seaside towns have been spoiled by urban spread and unsightly modern development.

Much of Tenby's 13th-century town wall is still intact, and the narrow streets, freshly recobbled to imitate days past, are still packed tight with shops and eating-houses of all shapes and sizes. On Castle Hill, at the head of the rocky promontory on which Tenby is spectacularly perched, stands the Albert Memorial, a towering Victorian monument unveiled in 1865 by

Tudor Square, Tenby

Prince Arthur. Albert looks down over Tenby's colourful and picturesque harbour - far and away the resort's most photographed, and therefore most recognisable, feature. Now here our Victorian time travellers would spot the difference, because in their day Tenby harbour was dominated by the boats of a thriving fishing industry, as opposed to the fleet of cruisers which in summer months now takes thousands of visitors to Caldey Island.

Tenby is unusual too in that its cliff top location means that the town itself has no through road. There are plenty of car parks outside the town walls, but in the old town pedestrians are far more comfortable and welcomed than are motorists. Walking is in

Tenby

Five Arches, Tenby

Tenby harbour by night

any case much more conducive to browsing in the shops and market and taking in the atmosphere of this ancient and charming town.

There is one other aspect of Tenby which the Victorians would still approve of - the magnificent beaches. The bathing machines have long since gone, but the superb stretches of golden sand remain with excellent facilities on hand at both North Beach and South Beach. The majority of the town's holiday accommodation, be it caravan parks, guest houses, hotels, or self-catering cottages and apartments, is also within easy striking distance of the beaches.

Away from the beach, Tenby has a great deal to show you. Here is a brief guide to some of the resort's most popular attractions.

Tenby Leisure Centre: See page 159.

Tenby Mural: Described as a panorama of Tenby history, this magnificent mural by local artist Eric Bradforth is a highly decorative and informative work of art gracing Tenby's refurbished Market Hall. The dimensions alone - 32 feet long by 8 feet deep - are impressive enough. Even a brief study reveals a wealth of detail about Tenby's past, including the building of the town walls, the opening of the Royal Victoria Pier in 1899, Mayor White helping Henry Tudor to escape to France in 1471, the arrival of the Pembroke and Tenby Railway in July 1863, and a great deal more.

A measure of Eric Bradforth's deep affection for Pembrokeshire where he has lived for more than 40 years, this stunning mural is definitely history at its most colourful. A detailed explanation of the painting's historical content is available by visiting Tenby Museum & Art Gallery. For further information ring 01834 842809.

Tenby Museum & Gallery: See page 148.

Castle Hill: Overlooking Tenby harbour, and with panoramic views across Carmarthen Bay to Worms Head on the Gower Peninsula, Castle Hill on a fine summers day is a wonderful place to unwind. It is also where you will find the Welsh national memorial to Prince Albert, Consort to Queen Victoria, which was inaugurated by Prince Arthur in August 1865. Another tribute to the Victorians is the replica bandstand, built in 1991, in which regular musical performances are given in summer months.

Tenby Harbour: Small, picturesque and brightly coloured by the neat painted cottages and spectrum of summer sail, Tenby harbour has a magnetic attraction. To sit on the harbour pier watching

Tudor Merchant's House

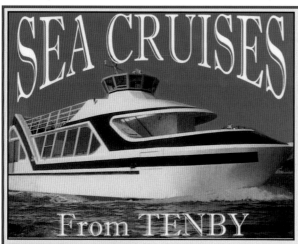

Tenby Harbour

fishermen cast their lines and the Caldey boats arriving and departing is certainly a very pleasurable way to do nothing. Alternatively, you could explore the lifeboat station, passing Laston House on the way, where in the 19th century Sir William Paxton established his baths and assembly rooms and helped put Tenby on the map as 'a fair and fashionable resort'.

Tudor Merchant's House: Owned and managed by the National Trust, Tenby's famous 15th-century Tudor Merchant's House is the oldest furnished residence in the town. It stands on Quay Hill, between the harbour and Tudor Square, and the authentic furnishings and fittings recreate the atmosphere of the period and illustrate the style in which a successful Tudor merchant and his family would have lived. Three of the interior walls bear the remains of early frescoes. The house is open between April and October on weekdays and Sundays; it closes on Saturdays. For further information ring 01834 842279 or 01558 822800.

Tenby Lifeboat Station: Tenby has two lifeboats - the RFA Sir Galahad and the much smaller inshore inflatable, the Arthur and Georgina Stanley Taylor. The Sir Galahad is housed in the main boathouse on the eastern side of Castle Hill, which was established in 1852. It has

a souvenir shop and a detailed record of many of the 200-plus lives saved by the Station's boats and crews in over 140 years of sterling voluntary service. The station is open to visitors from mid-May to the end of September between 11.00 am and 4.00 pm, Mondays to Fridays. From the end of May till the end of August it opens additionally from 7.00 p.m. to 9.00 p.m, Sundays to Fridays.

Caldey Island: As befits an island which for more than 1500 years has had strong religious connections, Caldey is a place of great peace and tranquillity. The early history of the island dates back to 8,000 BC and it also has a stunning natural beauty and is completely unspoilt. It is owned by the Reformed Order of Cistercian monks, who lead their lives according to the austere rule of St. Benedict and attend seven services each day in the simple dignity of the monastry church - the first at 3.25 am! The monastry

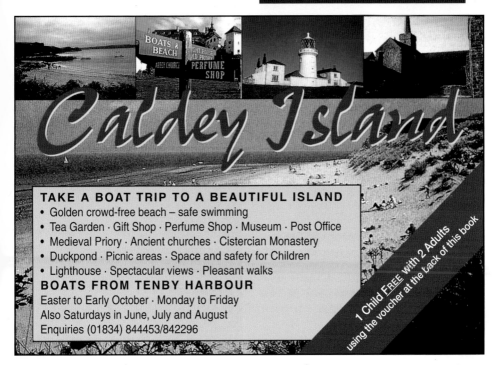

Caldey Island

TAKE A BOAT TRIP TO A BEAUTIFUL ISLAND
- Golden crowd-free beach – safe swimming
- Tea Garden · Gift Shop · Perfume Shop · Museum · Post Office
- Medieval Priory · Ancient churches · Cistercian Monastery
- Duckpond · Picnic areas · Space and safety for Children
- Lighthouse · Spectacular views · Pleasant walks

BOATS FROM TENBY HARBOUR
Easter to Early October · Monday to Friday
Also Saturdays in June, July and August
Enquiries (01834) 844453/842296

1 Child FREE with 2 Adults using the voucher at the back of this book

is the island's most obvious landmark; very Mediterranean in its architectural style and open to male visitors only. In addition to the many services they attend each day, the monks produce yoghurt, clotted cream, ice cream, chocolate and shortbread, as well as making hand lotion and perfumes inspired by the island's wild flowers. All are available from the gift shops on the island, where you will also find a post office and small museum, tea gardens, lighthouse, St. Illtud's church and the old Priory, and the beautiful sandy beach of Priory Bay, which is safe for bathing. Caldey and its small neighbouring island of St. Margaret's are home to a rich variety of birds and wildlife, including the Atlantic grey seal.

The island's full range of products is also on sale in the Caldey Island shop on Quay Hill, Tenby.

How to get there: A fleet of boats run to the island from Easter to October. Tickets are obtained from the Caldey Island kiosk at the top of Tenby harbour.

The ticket price includes return boat fare and landing fee and you can travel and return on any boat.

Boats run every 15 minutes between 9.30am and 5.00pm, Monday to Friday and also Saturdays from mid-May to mid-September. The island is closed on Sundays. The crossing time is about 20 minutes.

Caldey Island Shop, Quay Hill, Tenby: Perhaps the most interesting of their business ventures! The monks manufacture a famous range of Caldey perfumes and toiletries, inspired by the profusion of wild flowers, gorse and herbs. The islands full range of products are on sale at the shop, which also include dairy products, confectionrry and postcards.

De Valence Pavilion: Situated in Upper Frog Street, in the heart of the town, this impressive 500-seater hall hosts a great variety of entertainment throughout the year, from pop and rock concerts to local school performances to drama to fashion shows. It is also home to Stagestruck Productions, Tenby's very own amateur dramatics company, whose excellent offerings since its formation in 1989 include the musicals Oklahoma, Fiddler On The Roof, Annie Get Your Gun, Carousel, Guys 'N' Dolls, South Pacific and Brigadoon. For more details of the full 2000 programme of entertainment and events at the De Valence Pavilion, ring 01834 842730.

Silent World Aquarium: This aquarium and wildlife art gallery contains over 100 species of fish and other creatures. For more information ring 01834 844498.

Penally

Just west of Tenby, and well served by local trains, is the pretty hillside village of Penally. This enjoys a superb location, overlooking Tenby's golf course and South Beach, and from the station car park there is a very enjoyable walk across the links and dunes to the uncrowded western end of the beach. From here you can walk along the sands to Tenby. Or head in the other direction, towards Giltar Point, and explore a spectacular section of the Pembrokeshire Coastal Path, discovering such delights as Lydstep Haven.

Penally is a well-kept village, with a pottery, post office, shops, pubs, and a good choice of accommodation, including first-class hotel and camping and caravan sites. There is also a 6th-century Celtic cross, and in the 13th-century church of St. Nicholas a memorial to the victims of the Tenby lifeboat who drowned when it capsized in 1834.

Penally's proximity to Tenby, Lydstep, Manorbier, Freshwater East and Pembroke makes the village an ideal holiday base.

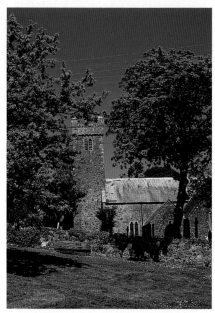

Penally Church

Other attractions nearby include Hoyles Mouth Cave and Ritec Valley Buggies.

St. Florence

Once a medieval harbour standing on an inlet to the sea, St. Florence is a picturesque village of great charm. It is a past winner of the national 'Wales In Bloom' competition, and boasts many pretty cottages. Here you will also discover one of the area's last surviving curious round chimneys, which are often described as Flemish in style. Also of interest is the 13th-century parish church, featuring a Norman tower. Located just 4 miles from Tenby.

St. Florence Cheese, Ivy Tower Farm:

At Ivy Tower Farm in the charming Pembrokeshire Village of St. Florence, Gaynor and Peter Quinn make a cheese to a recipe that has barely altered since medieval times - from the days when pilgrims would journey through the area bound for St. David's or the monastery on Caldey Island. A comprehensive range of cheese is made on the premises and there is something to suit every palate from our Cheshire style (natural or flavoured) to a Blue, a Soft (natural or smoked) a Wensleydale style (natural or herb & garlic) and a Goats' milk cheese.

Local milk is used for the cheese together with vegetarian rennet and the avoidance of artificial additives. Each cheese is individually bandaged in cheesecloth and matured on wooden shelves to produce the characteristic texture and flavour of traditional cheese. Our smokehouse is also on the premises and fruitwood from our own trees is used to produce the distinctive smoked flavour.

Visitors are welcome to watch the cheesemaking process and to taste the finished product. In addition to St. Florence cheese the shop keeps a selection of other local cheeses and dairy produce. In the licensed coffee shop you can choose from a selection of home-made pastries, morning coffee, afternoon tea, ploughman's lunches, cold drinks, ice cream sundaes, wines and the like for your refreshment and enjoyment.

Directions: OS ref. SN084016. Turn towards village off the B4318 (Tenby/Sageston). We are about 100 yards past the 30mph sign on the left hand side of the road.

Opening: Shop and coffee shop Monday-Friday 10.00am/6.00pm. Saturday 9.00am/4.00pm. Easter to end of September. Sundays 10.00am/4.00pm - bank holidays and summer. Cheese is usually made from about 10.00am/1.00pm Monday, Wednesday & Friday in the early spring and autumn; daily throughout late spring and summer. Facilities: Cheese making, shop, licensed coffee shop, toilets, parking.

Great Wedlock Dinosaur Experience, Gumfreston: For more information ring 01834 845272.

Heatherton Country Sports Park, St. Florence: See page 140.

Manor House Wildlife & Leisure Park, St. Florence: For more information ring 01834 871952.

Saundersfoot

This bustling village resort is about three miles from Tenby, lying at the foot of a picturesque wooded valley. With its attractive harbour and extensive sandy beaches, Saundersfoot has established itself as a popular centre for sailing, fishing, water-sports and traditional seaside holidays. It is also very well placed as a base for exploring Pembrokeshire's south coast.

Originally a small fishing village and home to two shipyards by the 1800's, Saundersfoot was suddenly caught up in the excitement of the black gold rush when high-quality anthracite was discovered locally. Such was the demand for this coal that in 1829 the harbour was built, connected by rail to six mines. The railway ran along what is now The Strand, and the coal was exported worldwide. It was not until the start of the Second World War that coal shipments ceased, but by this time another flourishing industry was putting the village on the map - tourism.

The parish church of Saundersfoot, St. Issells, dates from the 13th century and is located in a beautiful position just outside the village. Saundersfoot also gives access by the coastal path to the headland of Monkstone Point. Further along the path, towards Tenby, you will find the small and sandy cove of Waterwynch, with a delightful and well-appointed hotel.

Amroth

The small coastal village of Amroth sits on the Pembrokeshire-Carmarthenshire border, just 7 miles from Tenby and 4 miles from Saundersfoot. It is a wild and beautifully unspoilt location. In summer the wonderful expanse of gently shelving sand, exposed at low tide, makes it a

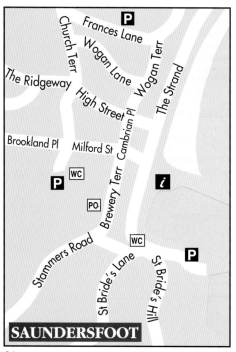

SAUNDERSFOOT

Saundersfoot

favourite beach for families and anglers alike. The village, spread along the narrow seafront, lacks the frills of bigger resorts but has plenty of good facilities - including restaurants, pubs, gift shops, caravan parks and holiday homes - and an undeniable charm. Amroth also marks the southern end, or starting point, of the 186-mile Pembrokeshire Coastal Path (the northern end being at Poppit Sands). Attractions close by include Colby Woodland Garden, which is owned by the National Trust, and Pendine Sands - a resort made famous in the 1920's by speed king Sir Malcolm Campbell.

Wisemans Bridge

This tiny hamlet, best known for its inn and rocky beach, nestles on the coast road between Saundersfoot and Amroth, and at low tide it is possible to walk across the sands to either. You can also walk to Saundersfoot through the tunnels that were once part of the railway link between local mines and Saundersfoot harbour. In 1944 Winston Churchill was present here, witnessing rehearsals for the D-Day landings in Normandy.

Just inland from Wiseman's Bridge is modestly named 'Pleasant Valley'. This beautiful wooded vale, which is ideal country, leads to Stepaside and well worth seeing.

Stepaside

Stepaside is accessible either via Wiseman's Bridge, which takes you through Pleasant Valley, or from Kilgetty village or bypass. It is hard to believe it now, but in the 19th century this quiet little hamlet was a hive of industry after the Pembrokeshire Iron and Coal Company built the Kilgetty Ironworks here in 1848. Iron ore, in plentiful supply from seams along the cliffs between Amroth and Saundersfoot, was smelted in the blast

Wisemans Bridge

furnace using locally produced limestone and coal and the iron was transported to Saundersfoot harbour by the railway built for the anthracite mines. However from the outset, the ironworks were beset by major problems, and it ceased operations less than forty years after going into production.

This chapter in the area's industrial history is recorded in detail in the fascinating Stepaside Heritage Centre, which is one of several interesting attractions here. Others are the Stepaside Bird and Animal Park, craft workshops, picnic areas, a woodland walk and other features, which make for a very enjoyable visit.

Stepaside Bird & Animal Park: The unusual and fascinating species of birds, mammals and reptiles you will find here are not those typically on show in other parks. For further information ring 01834 811710 or 843102.

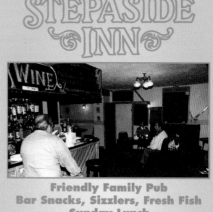

Saundersfoot Bay Leisure Park

PRINCE OF WALES AWARD

Best Caravan Park in Britain - **CALOR** *Gas Award 1994*

Please 'phone or call in for a colour brochure

Saundersfoot Bay Leisure Park,
Saundersfoot, Pembrokeshire
SA69 9DG

Telephone: (01834) 812284
Fax: (01834) 813387

Email: saundersfoot.bay@business.ntl.com
Web: www.saundersfootbay.co.uk

DRAGON AWARD

Situated on the beautiful Pembrokeshire National Park coastline between Saundersfoot and Tenby, about 10 minutes stroll from the beach, this award-winning park commands magnificent views over Carmarthen Bay. Our top quality holiday homes are fully equipped and every unit has full mains services, heating throughout, microwave oven, fridge/freezer and colour TV with video player. A free video library is available on site.

New and used holiday homes for sale on site. Finance arranged if required.

What the experts say

Wales Tourist Board "Excellent"
Pembrokeshire Coast National Park "Outstanding, highly commended"
Wales in Bloom "Beautifully private and screened from the world"
Prince of Wales Award "Something very special"
Horticulture Week "No ordinary caravan park"

Colby Woodland Garden: Described by the National Trust as one of their most beautiful properties in Pembrokeshire, this garden is part of the Colby Estate, which was established by the 19th-century-mining entrepreneur John Colby. The garden is a spectacular blaze of colour from early spring to the end of June. On site is a National Trust shop, along with gallery, plant sales, toilets and a car park. For more information ring 01834 811885.

Kilgetty

Before the bypass was built, the main road into South Pembrokeshire from the east went through Kilgetty village. But Kilgetty remains an important centre for visitors, with its Tourist Information Centre, railway station, supermarket and shops, and it is close to several major attractions. The neighbouring village of Begelly, for example, is well known for both Folly Farm and Begelly Pottery and a short distance west of Kilgetty are the villages of Broadmoor and East Williamston, where there are first-class caravan parks, a pub, and a garage offering cycle hire. Approximately 2 miles from Saundersfoot, Kilgetty is mid-way between Narberth and Tenby and only half a mile from Stepaside.

Folly Farm, Begelly: See page 142.

Manorbier

Manorbier is a small seaside village midway between Tenby and Pembroke, and best known for two striking features - the beach, which at low tide reveals a beautiful sandy cove, and the well-preserved medieval castle. The castle enjoys a spectacular location overlooking the bay, and from its towers the views are magnificent. Within these walls was born Gerald of Wales, a much-respected medieval writer and man of many talents, whose two major works are still in print to

Colby Lodge

A DAY OUT
at
Manorbier
Castle
and beach

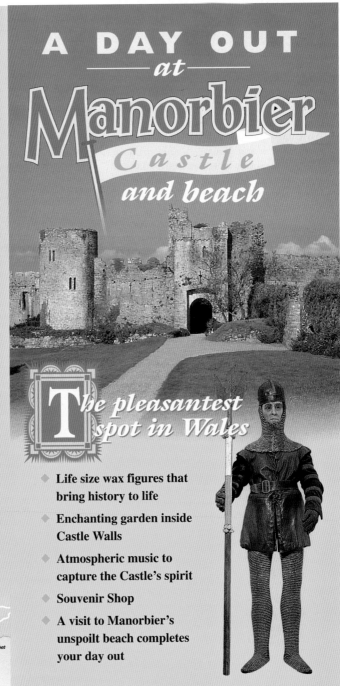

With such a splendid setting overlooking a beautiful unspoilt beach, families love to explore Manorbier Castle and bring a little bit of history to life.

The impressive Great Hall, Chapel and Turrets are dotted with life size figures – see children of the Tudor period and some prisoners in the dungeon.

Look out for Gerald of Wales – the great twelfth century scholar who was born here, and described the Castle as "the pleasantest spot in Wales."

The car park is conveniently situated between the Castle and the beach, so you can enjoy a great family day out at the Castle **and** one of Pembrokeshire's loveliest beaches.

Opening times:
Daily from Easter to 30 September
10.30am to 5.30pm

Admission:
£2.00 adults
£1.00 children and senior citizens
Dogs admitted only on a lead. Picnics welcomed.
Excellent local transport:-
Bus no. 358
Tenby-Haverfordwest stops at the gate.
Train station ¾ mile away

The pleasantest spot in Wales

- Life size wax figures that bring history to life
- Enchanting garden inside Castle Walls
- Atmospheric music to capture the Castle's spirit
- Souvenir Shop
- A visit to Manorbier's unspoilt beach completes your day out

39

this day. Gerald was not the only writer to find inspiration in Manorbier: George Bernard Shaw spent several months here and prior to her marriage in 1912 Virginia Woolf was a regular summer visitor. Close to the castle, on the opposite side of the vale, is the impressive Norman church of St. James. Manorbier beach is very popular with surfers and summer holidaymakers, and the facilities in the village include a post office, hotel and a cosy pub serving good food. Skrinkle Haven, one of South Pembrokeshire's most sheltered and beautiful beaches, is also close to the village. A short walk along the coast path takes you to Swanlake Bay, yet another sandy beach.

Manorbier Castle

The Bier House: The Bier House is in the centre of the village. It was built in 1900 to house the parish bier - a funeral cart that was used to carry the dead to the burial ground. The building has recently been restored and now provides an information point relating to the history of the parish.

Lamphey

The village of Lamphey is about two miles east of Pembroke, on the A4139 Tenby-Pembroke road. The Bishops of St. David's built a palace here in the 13th century, the ruins of which are now in the care of Cadw (Welsh Historic Monuments). On land adjacent to the palace stands an impressive colonnaded building, originally a fine Georgian house. The village is also well known for its hospitality. At the Lamphey Hall Hotel, for example, all rooms are en suite and there is a bistro open all year round, in addition to the restaurant. Lamphey has its own railway station and is easily accessible by rail from Pembroke, Tenby and Saundersfoot. Less than two miles south of

the village is the popular beach of Freshwater East.

Lamphey Bishop's Palace: Located less than two miles from Pembroke, on the edge of Lamphey village, the remains of

40

the spectacular 13th-century Bishop's Palace are an evocative reminder of the great power enjoyed by the medieval bishops of St. David's. The comfortable palace buildings were set among well-stocked fishponds, plump orchards and an extensive vegetable garden, and Lamphey boasted an impressive 144-acre park, a deer herd, a windmill, two watermills and a dovecote. The palace's finest architectural features included the great hall, built by Bishop Henry de Gower in the 14th century, and the 16th-century chapel. The ruins are open all the time between October 1st and April 30th, and daily from 10.00 am to 5.30 p.m. from May 28th to September 30th. For more information ring the Pembroke Tourist Information & Visitor Centre on 01646 622388, or CADW (Welsh Historic Monuments) on 01222 465511.

Manorbier

Pembroke

Distances: Fishguard 26, Haverfordwest 10, Milford Haven 5, Narberth 15, St. David's 26, Tenby 12, Carmarthen 32 and London 252.

Pembroke is a small but charming walled town with a genteel atmosphere and a 900-year history, and it has much to commend it to visitors.

Like so many other Welsh towns, Pembroke grew up around its medieval castle. This magnificent structure, birthplace of Henry VII, enjoys a spectacular location and is in a very good state of preservation - the result of an extensive programme of restoration that was started in 1928. The castle, described more fully on page 45, demands a visit: for the fitter and more agile members of the family, the breathtaking views from the top of the famous round keep are a treat not to be missed.

The vast majority of Pembroke's shops, banks, restaurants and many of its most impressive Georgian houses, are to be found along Main Street - a pleasant thoroughfare with facades ranging from Tudor to modern. Here you will discover an interesting mix of retail outlets, along with a Pembrokeshire Coast National Park Information Centre, a National Trust shop and a variety of visitor attractions that include the novel and fascinating Museum of the Home. Also close to Main Street is the superb Pembroke Visitor Centre. This incorporates the Tourist Information Centre and an imaginative display that depicts aspects of the town's long history.

Running parallel with Main Street, on its northern side, is the Mill Pond, formed by one of the two tidal creeks, which helped give Pembroke Castle its excellent

Pembroke Castle

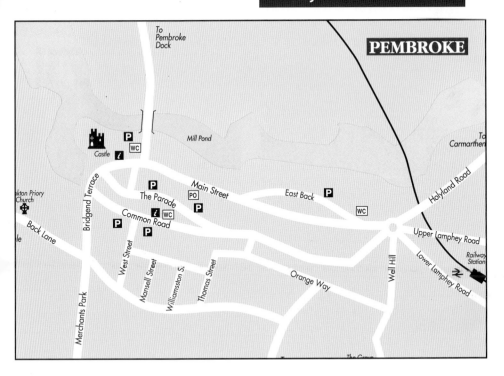

PEMBROKE

Pembroke Castle

High on a cliff face on the bank of the River Cleddau, overlooking the historic town and its Mill Pond, Pembroke Castle, the oldest in West Wales, is an imposing sight. Dating back to the thirteenth century, the castle is one of the foremost examples of Norman architecture in Wales, and its five-storey, 75 feet high circular Keep, or Great Tower, is the finest of its type in Britain.

Home to such great personalities as Earl William Marshal, Regent to Henry III, and and the early Tudors the castle boasts the birth of a King within its walls - Henry VII or "Harri" Tudor

Exhibitions, displays and videos give a fascinating insight into both county history and national heritage. NEW - a superb tableau depicting`, Lady Margaret Beaufort with her new born son the Earl of Richmond, later to become Henry VII.

OPENING HOURS

The Castle is open to the public daily at the following times

I April - 30 Sept (inc. Sun)	9.30am - 6.00pm
March & Oct (inc. Sun)	10.00am - 5.00pm
Nov to Feb (inc. Sun)	10.00am - 4.00pm

The Castle is closed to the public on 24th, 25th, and 26th December.

ENTRANCE FEES 2000

Adults	£3.00
Concessions	£2.00
Family Tickets (2 adults + 2 children under 16)	£8.00
Children under 5 and disabled (in wheelchairs)	FREE
Parties of 20 or more	£2.60 & £1.70

Guided tours by arrangement daily (except Sats) from end May to end August (additional charge 50p per person). Children under 16 free). Snack Bar open Summer months

Further Information:
Pembroke Castle Trust, Pembroke SA71 4LA
Tel Office: 01646 681510   Ticket Office 01646 684585

birthplace of the Tudor dynasty

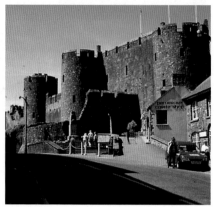

Pembroke

Main Street, Pembroke

defensive position. On a fine day Mill Pond Walk is a favourite beauty spot with locals and visitors alike. Swans, herons, cormorants and, on rare occasions, even otters can be seen along this peaceful stretch of water.

Throughout the year Pembroke and the castle are the venue for many important events, several of which are traditions rooted firmly in the town's medieval past.

After the Normans arrived here in 1093, the town became the base from which they increased their hold on West Wales. Pembroke developed as a major market centre, with regular fairs and markets held in the wide, single street near the castle - now Main Street. One of the most important of these gatherings was the annual hiring fair in which shepherds,

cowherds and labourers lined the street to persuade farmers to employ them for the following year. This tradition is still remembered. The Pembroke Fair, held every October, is a very popular event that brings rides, amusements and all the fun of the fair to Main Street.

Pembroke Castle also hosts many such attractions, including Shakespearean productions, medieval banquets, military tattoos and displays by the Sealed Knot Society. Every year the Cleddau Festival culminates in Pembroke Castle with a spectacular August firework display.

In the best Welsh tradition, Pembroke boasts two excellent choirs - the Pembroke Male Voice Choir and the Griffon Choir -, both of that perform regularly in the town.

As you explore Pembroke, you will see much evidence of the town's ancient and extensive walls. These are a throwback to the 13th century, when the townsfolk demanded that stone walls be built to protect their cottages from raiders. (Although the castle was virtually impenetrable, any building that lay outside the castle walls was at the mercy of unwelcome visitors.) To complete the building of the town walls took 30 years. There were three gates - east, west and north - of which only a fragment of the Westgate now remains. However, large sections of wall still survive.

Throughout the 900 years since the Norman Conquest, Pembroke has experienced fluctuating fortunes. Under Norman rule, the town' s position on the Haven Waterway established it as an important trading port. Coal, wool, wheat, lime, cloth, leather and other goods were shipped to ports all around the British coast and exported to Ireland, France, Spain and Portugal. Maritime trade flourished between the 17th and 19th centuries - until the railway arrived. The gradual silting up of the shallow river entrance to Pembroke compounded such tough competition, and the prosperity of the once-wealthy port began to dwindle.

By the end of the Second World War the town was relatively poor and was overlooked for large-scale redevelopment. Although unhelpful to the local economy, this was not entirely a bad thing, as in 1977 Pembroke was designated an Outstanding Conservation Area. Today it remains beautifully unspoilt and continues to attract large numbers of visitors from all over the world.

Pembroke also makes for an ideal holiday base - one of the four main tourist centres of South Pembrokeshire. This is the gateway to the Castlemartin Peninsula, which though wild and remote is home to

Europe's biggest oil refinery. This giant petrochemical plant fills the skyline at Rhoscrowther, near Angle, just seven miles from Pembroke. Yet even the refinery's presence cannot hide a fascinating landscape, remarkable coastline and a wonderful diversity of birds and wildlife. To miss the Castlemartin Peninsula is to miss one of Pembrokeshire's most interesting facets.

By the same token, to miss Pembroke and its wonderfully atmospheric castle is to miss one of Britain's most historic towns.

Museum of the Home: A novel museum housing a unique collection of more than 3000 everyday items that represent all the facets of domestic life as it used to be. The museum, opposite Pembroke Castle, is open from the beginning of May until the end of September, Monday to Thursday inclusive. For more information ring 01646 681200.

Pembroke Visitor Centre: Built to coincide with the town's 900th birthday celebrations in 1993, this attraction is an integral part of Pembroke's superb new Tourist Information Centre on Commons Road, below Main Street. As well as an interesting video, you can see displays and exhibits that tell the story of Pembroke, and fun items to delight the younger members of the family. There is also an attractive choice of gifts, books, maps and souvenirs on sale. For more details, or for tourist information, ring 01646 622388.

Pembroke Castle: Birthplace of Henry VII and one of the best-preserved medieval castles in Wales, Pembroke is open to visitors all year round and is an intriguing place to explore. Its wide walls are honeycombed with a seemingly endless system of rooms, passageways and spiralling flights of narrow stone steps;

interpretative displays and information panels give a fascinating insight into the castle's origins and long history. One of the most impressive features is the distinctive round keep, which was built soon after 1200. It is 75 feet high and the views from the top in all directions are nothing less than magnificent.

From this lofty position it is very easy to understand why the Normans, who came to Pembroke in 1093, were well aware that the site was ideal for fortification - a low rocky peninsula between two tidal creeks, offering superb natural defences. They quickly established a wooden fortress, and in 1200 began work on the castle itself - the impressive stone structure we see today. Pembroke became the main Norman base in West Wales and a town quickly grew up around the castle to serve its many needs.

Harri Tudor (Henry VII) was born in Pembroke Castle on 28th January 1457 of an Anglesey family. In 1485 he returned from exile in France, landing at Millbay on the Milford Haven waterway. From here he marched a growing army of largely untrained volunteers across country to Bosworth Field in Leicestershire to confront Richard III. Against the odds, Henry's heavily outnumbered forces defeated Richard and Henry became King of England. So ended the Wars of the Roses and began the Tudor dynasty.

Today, Pembroke Castle is the region's most famous historic landmark and one of Wales' greatest visitor attractions. Of particular interest is the Exhibition Room. Here you can see an introductory video and a display that records the history of the Pembroke Yeomanry and the story of the last invasion of mainland Britain in 1797.

Pembroke Dock

Just two miles from Pembroke is Pembroke Dock, which stands on the Milford Haven waterway. From here you can head west to Ireland on the daily Pembroke Dock-Rosslare ferry, passing the town of Milford Haven itself - Britain's busiest oil port. Or you can go east and get acquainted with the many charms of the Daugleddau River and its mysterious tidal creeks, often referred to as South Pembrokeshire's secret waterway.

Pembroke and Pembroke Dock are alike in only one respect: both have experienced fluctuating fortunes. There the similarity ends, because as a place of any significance Pembroke Dock has a very short history.

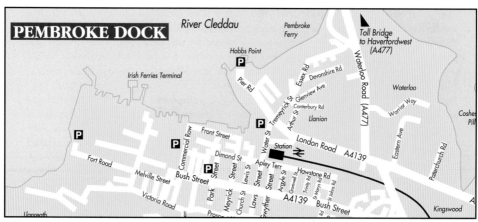

In the early 19th century it was nothing more than a small coastal village known as Paterchurch. But when in 1814 the lease expired on the Royal Naval Dockyard in Milford Haven, the Admiralty decided to move its shipbuilding operation across the water and further inland from the mouth of the estuary - and Paterchurch was designated the ideal site. Hence began an amazing transformation, which saw naval architects lay out the distinctive grid pattern of wide streets so characteristic of present-day Pembroke Dock. The prosperous new town grew up around the thriving dockyard, and many fine ships were built here. These included HMS Tartar, the first steam man-of-war; HMS Conflict, the first propeller-driven warship and several royal yachts.

When the dockyard closed in 1926 it had produced more than 260 ships, and the town's population exceeded 3000. But it was not long before ships were replaced by a totally different kind of boat. In 1930 a major part of the dockyard site was transferred from the Admiralty to the Air Ministry, and in the following year the Royal Air Force established a seaplane base, operated by Southampton flying boats of 210 Squadron. 1938 saw the arrival of the squadron's first Sunderland flying boat - the aircraft with which Pembroke Dock is most associated, for during the Second World War the Sunderlands gave sterling service and eventually stayed on here until 1957. Even today the Sunderland is far from forgotten, and on occasions its spirit is revived in startling fashion. In March 1993, for example, during one of the lowest tides of the century, three men discovered the remains of a rear gun turret and fairing - part of a Sunderland flying boat of 201 Squadron that crashed in the Haven waterway during a training exercise in March 1954.

Pembroke Dock

Today, Pembroke Dock is better known for its supermarket, shops, library, ferry port, excellent boating and watersport facilities, and the new Martello Guntower Visitor Centre, which traces the history of the unique network of defences along the Haven waterway and Western Approaches.

There are also interesting walks - most notably the town trail and the Cleddau toll bridge, which, at 150 feet high, gives spectacular views over the waterway in both directions. The Cleddau Bridge is, in fact, a very significant landmark. Because once you have crossed it to the waterway's northern shore you have left South Pembrokeshire behind.

The Gun Tower Visitor Centre: Opened in 1995, this visitor centre is built within one of the 19th-century towers that formed part of the fortifications of the Milford Haven waterway. The tower's specific role was to help defend and protect the Royal Naval dockyard, though in the event the only threat came from air raids in the Second World War - long after the dockyard had closed. The tower, completed in 1851, also incorporates a new Tourist Information Centre. Admission is free. For more information ring 01646 622246.

The Castlemartin Peninsula

The Castlemartin Peninsula, which is also known as the Angle Peninsula, typifies the unique appeal of South Pembrokeshire in that it has many special features of interest to many different groups.

The magnificent scenery which unfolds along the coast path, and the profusion of wild flowers and butterflies to be found here captivates sightseers, walkers, photographers, artists and naturalists.

Birdwatchers flock here for the colonies of guillemots, razorbills, kittiwakes, choughs and other species that nest along the cliffs and rock formations.

To geologists, the peninsula presents some outstanding examples of fissures, sea caves, blowholes, natural arches and stacks - the result of continual sea erosion of the carboniferous limestone cliffs.

St Govan's Head looking east

Anthropologists have been excited by the discovery of bones and implements in caves which 20,000 years ago gave shelter to the region's earliest-known human inhabitants.

Historians are enchanted by such mysteries as tiny St. Govan's Chapel and by the remains of Iron Age forts and other ancient sites.

And for visitors who are here simply to enjoy a holiday, there are attractions such as the Bosherston lily ponds and the superb beaches of Barafundle, Broad Haven, Freshwater West and West Angle Bay to savour.

The Castlemartin Peninsula is also famous (though many would say infamous) for its 6000-acre Ministry of Defence tank range. This means that a large section of coastline is inaccessible - one of the very few places where the Pembrokeshire Coastal Path is diverted inland - but there is some compensation to visitors, in that on certain days a spectator area enables you to

Looking towards Grenala Point

watch the tanks in action as they fire live ammunition at a variety of still and moving targets.

Much of the southern half of the peninsula, including the tank range, was once part of the Stackpole Estate. This embraced more than 13,000 acres and was one of the most substantial land holdings in Wales. Until 1688 the estate was owned by the Lort family of Stackpole, but in that year it changed hands when Elizabeth Lort married Alexander Campbell of the Cawdor Estate in Scotland. It was the enterprising Campbells who created the Bosherston lakes and lily ponds. They also planted a great variety of trees and introduced many unusual and innovative ideas to the estate, including the building of a stone icehouse - an 18th-century refrigerator in which dairy produce was stored. In 1976 the National Trust acquired 2000 acres of the estate and is now responsible for its management. Sadly, though, the mansion that stood on the estate - Stackpole Court - was demolished in the 1960's.

Like Pembrokeshire itself, the Castlemartin Peninsula has a certain isolated charm and magic - qualities that set it apart and beg exploration.

Freshwater East

From the small coastal village of Freshwater East, which has a fine sandy beach backed by low dunes and flanked by red sandstone cliffs, you are ideally placed to explore the stunning coastline of the Castlemartin Peninsula. Stackpole Quay, Barafundle Bay, the Bosherston lily ponds and Broad Haven beach are all within very easy reach along the coast path, while only Barafundle is inaccessible by road. Freshwater East is also a popular resort in its own right. The Trewent Park holiday complex provides self-catering accommodation close to the beach, and

St Govan's Head

there are shops, a touring caravan park and other facilities. A major road improvement scheme has also been undertaken in the last couple of years. With Pembroke and Pembroke Dock both close at hand, this attractive resort offers the dual benefit of a peaceful setting and convenient shopping and other amenities.

Stackpole

Stackpole has its name in Norse origins, and the village as it stands today is in a different place from its original medieval site, having been moved by the Campbells in 1735 to accommodate growth of the Stackpole Estate. The centre of the old village is about half a mile to the southwest, marked by the remains of a preaching cross.

Close to the present village are interesting areas of woodland - Castle Dock, Cheriton Bottom, Caroline Grove and Lodge Park - which were planted as part of the estate 200 years ago. There are species here from all over the world, many of them brought in from London's Kew Gardens. The woods are managed by the National Trust, who have created several miles of pathways for horses and walkers.

St Govan's Chapel

Lily Ponds, Bosherston

The centre of attraction in Stackpole village is the Armstrong Arms, a welcoming country inn occupying a charming old building of 16th century origin.

Stackpole Quay

The National Trust owns and manages Stackpole Quay, which it acquired in 1976 as part of the 2000 acres of Stackpole Estate. This acquisition also included the stretch of coastline between here and Broad Haven, under the Enterprise Neptune initiative - a scheme launched by the Trust in 1965 to save and protect Britain's precious and threatened coastline.

Stackpole Quay was originally a private quay built for the estate, so that coal could be imported and limestone shipped out from the quarry. It is claimed that this is Britain's smallest harbour, however pleasure boats are now the only craft that use the stone jetty.

There are good parking facilities here, as well as toilets and a new National Trust information centre and cafe. This car park is as close as you can get by road to nearby Barafundle beach, which is accessible via the coast path.

Stackpole Quay is also notable for its geological features. Fossils of old shells and corals can be seen in the rocks, and just to the east of the quay is a change in the cliff landscape, where the grey carboniferous limestone gives way to deposits of old red sandstone.

Stackpole Quarry

As part of its management of the Stackpole Estate, the National Trust has utilised the natural geological features of the old quarry near Stackpole Quay to create an area in which visitors - including those with special needs - can enjoy countryside recreation. Around the top of the quarry is a circular path giving spectacular vistas of the surrounding landscape and coastline. Down below, on the quarry floor, are sheltered picnic and barbecue areas and an archery bay. In addition, the cleared rock faces present a challenge to experienced climbers and abseilers.

Everyone can use the quarry's facilities, but groups or event organisers should first contact the warden. Close to the quarry is the main car park for Stackpole Quay, along with National Trust holiday cottages, carefully converted from old buildings. For more information about holiday lets or the quarry facilities, ring the Trust's Stackpole office on 01646 661359.

Bosherston

For such a small village, Bosherston certainly enjoys a large share of fame. This

Lily Ponds, Bosherston

is due to its proximity for several major tourist attractions in South Pembrokeshire. These include the delightful Bosherston lily ponds - part of the Stackpole lakes - and Broad Haven beach. Pembroke is only 6 miles away. On days when the M.O.D tank range is not in use and the access roads are open, Bosherston is also the gateway to remarkable St. Govan's Chapel and some of the best limestone cliff scenery in Europe, with coastal features such as St. Govan's Head, Huntsman's Leap, Stack Rocks and the Green Bridge of Wales.

The village itself is not without interest. The name is believed to be a corruption of Bosher's tun, or farm.

14th-century St. Michael's Church has an unusual cross of the same period standing in the churchyard, and much older still is a huge boulder, originating from Scotland, which was deposited at Bosherston by a moving glacier during the last Ice Age.

Bosherston also has ample parking (with alternative parking above Broad Haven beach) and a pub, tearooms and toilets. When the tank range access road is open, there is also plenty of free parking at St. Govan's.

Whether you want to tread the coast path, laze on the beach, stroll round the lily ponds or simply enjoy a picnic in a beautiful setting, Bosherston is an excellent base for a great day out. To find out in advance when the range access roads will be open, ask at any Tourist or National Park Information Centre, or ring Merrion Camp direct on 01646 661321 or Bosherston Post Office on 01646 661286. Details are also published in the local press.

Bosherston Lily Ponds & Broad Haven Beach: When the Campbells of Stackpole created the lakes and lily ponds to enhance their estate in the late 18th and early 19th centuries, they were unwittingly setting the scene for an attraction that now

51

Castlemartin

Angle

brings thousands of annual visitors to the small village of Bosherston. Covering more than 80 acres, the lakes and lily ponds are the largest area of fresh water in the Pembrokeshire Coast National Park, and are part of the Stackpole National Nature Reserve. The lily ponds are usually at their very best around June, when the lilies are in full bloom, but even in winter they provide easy and fascinating walks. They also offer good coarse fishing and are well stocked with roach, pike, tench and eels. Fishing permits are available from the cafe in the village.

There are in fact three lakes, artificially created by the deliberate flooding of narrow limestone valleys. The lily ponds occupy only the western lake, which is fed by underwater springs. Grey herons are regular visitors, and the total lakes area attracts a great variety of birds and wildlife, including coots, moorhens, mallard, teal, swans, cormorants, kingfishers, buzzards, and many smaller winged visitors, such as blue damselflies and emperor dragonflies. Over 20 species of duck alone have been recorded here.

Leaving the car park and walking round the western lake in either direction brings you to Broad Haven beach and the coast path. Alternatively, you can continue to the eastern lake and discover the impressive 8-arch bridge and, a little

further on, the site of Stackpole Court - the former home of the Campbell family, a huge house demolished in the 1960's. Along the way you pass mixed deciduous woodland, planted by the estate in the 18th century and now an ideal habitat for greater spotted woodpecker and small woodland birds such as blackcap and chiffchaff.

The water from the three lakes (there is no access or footpath to the central lake) runs out on to Broad Haven beach through a rocky culvert and cuts a winding and fast-moving channel through the sand to the sea. This superb beach is backed by sand dunes, which are stabilised by marram grass - a plant that thrives in conditions inhospitable to most other species. These young dunes have accumulated since the end of the 18th century, when the three lakes were created, and are an environmentally sensitive area which visitors are asked to avoid.

On the eastern side of the beach the coast path rises towards Stackpole Head, and on the western side towards St. Govan's. From these headlands on a clear day you can see Lundy Island, off the North Devon coast, and Worms Head on the Gower Peninsula. The whole area around Bosherston is superb walking country, and even if your ambition is

The Green Bridge of Wales

Thorn Island

limited to a pleasant stroll, the lily ponds are an attraction not to be missed.

St.Govan's Chapel: Remarkable St. Govan' s Chapel is one of the wonders of Pembrokeshire. A tiny building hidden in a fissure in the cliff near St. Govan's car park, the restored chapel nestles at the bottom of a flight of narrow stone steps. It is said that if you count the steps on the way down and then count them on the way back up, the numbers won't tally! This is only one of the mysteries and legends attached to the chapel. Though it occupies the site of a 5th-century hermit's cell, the age of the chapel itself is not known for sure; expert estimates put it at no older than 11th-century. St. Govan is reputedly buried here beneath the altar, and it is also said that Sir Gawaine, one of King Arthur's knights, lived here in isolation. Yet another legend tells of the holy well's miraculous healing powers.

St. Govan's Chapel is close to St. Govan's Head - the most southerly point in Pembrokeshire, and well worth seeing for its dramatic cliff scenery. Both are accessible via the road that runs through Bosherston village.

Huntsman's Leap: According to legend, a horseman fleeing from pursuers miraculously leaped across this gaping chasm in the cliffs west of St. Govan's Chapel. On looking back he was so horrified by the prospect of what might have happened that the shock killed him anyway!

Castlemartin

In the small village of Castlemartin is a circular stone cattle pound, built in the 18th century, which now serves as a traffic roundabout. There is another connection here with cattle in that the land, rich and well drained because of the carboniferous limestone, is some of the most fertile in Wales and was at one time renowned for its high cereal yield and breed of Castlemartin Welsh Black cattle.

Close to the village is the tank range spectator area, which when open gives free admission to cars and coaches. Just east of Castlemartin is Merrion Camp itself, where two tanks stand on display at the main gates. When the range is not in use there is access to Stack Rocks car park. From here it is only a short walk to the spectacular Green Bridge of Wales - a natural limestone arch - and the two vertical rock stacks that give rise to the name Stack Rocks. In early summer these rocks are a cacophony of calling seabirds as thousands of breeding guillemots and razorbills cling to every ledge, nook and cranny.

Flimston Chapel

This medieval chapel, used as a barn until it was restored, is now open to visitors and stands beside a deserted farm on the Castlemartin tank range. It is accessible along the road to Stack Rocks car park (which is open only when the range is not in use). It is dedicated to St. Martin, and in the churchyard, where boulders deposited by glaciers have been used as gravestones, stands the stone Ermigate Cross.

Stack Rocks

Also known as the Elegug Stacks, these two tall pinnacles of rock standing close to the cliffs at Stack Rocks car park are literally bursting with life in early summer, when they are home to thousands of nesting guillemots, razorbills, kittiwakes, fulmars and gulls. The name Elegug is South Pembrokeshire dialect and a corruption of heligog, which is the Welsh word for guillemot.

Green Bridge of Wales

Standing just 150 yards or so from Stack Rocks car park, the Green Bridge of Wales is an excellent example of a natural

Castlemartin Church

limestone arch. It was formed by the joining of two caves, each created by erosion of the rock through constant bombardment by the sea, and eventually the roof of the arch will collapse and leave

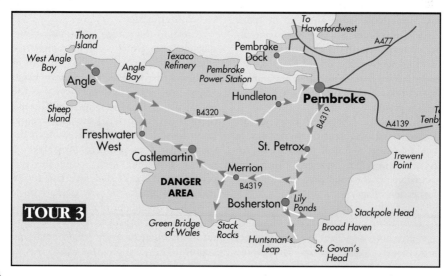

TOUR 3

Angle Bay

a pinnacle of rock - a stack - standing in the sea. This is the same process that created Stack Rocks. The Green Bridge of Wales is easy to see and photograph in full profile - with complete safety - thanks to the wooden viewing platform constructed specially for the purpose by the National Park Authority.

Angle

The village of Angle, sandwiched between the popular sandy beach of West Angle Bay and the pleasure craft which moor in East Angle Bay, is 8 miles west of Pembroke at the entrance to the Milford Haven waterway, and has a long seafaring tradition. It also has a lifeboat, housed in an impressive modern station, and a number of interesting features. Among its historic buildings are a medieval fortified residence (known as the Tower House), the scant remains of a castle, a dovecote, and 15th-century Angle Hall. Also surviving are long, narrow fields which are rare examples of the strip system of farming which the Normans introduced in the late Middle Ages.

Angle and the surrounding area is superb walking country. In addition to the delights to be discovered on the coast path, there is much to see along the Haven waterway, where giant supertankers and small sailing dinghies share an unlikely co-existence in one of the world's best natural deep-water harbours.

The beach at West Angle Bay, along with those of Broad Haven (south), Barafundle and Freshwater West, is described in the beach guide in the first chapter.

Readers who wish to explore the area are recommended to follow Tour 3 in this guide - see page 185 and for map information see overleaf.

Haverfordwest & the West Coast

Pembrokeshire's Atlantic West Coast is a wild and dramatic landscape of spectacular cliff scenery, golden beaches and secluded coves. Offshore are the nearby islands of Skomer and Skokholm and, much further out to sea, Grassholm - names which are a reminder of the days when ransacking Viking war lords and Norse settlers made their mark in the area.

In terms of resorts, this coastline has nothing to compare with Tenby for size and general amenities - a fact which makes it all the more appealing to those visitors in search of peaceful isolation. Even here there are popular village resorts, such as Broad Haven and Dale, which, though small and very relaxing, are only a few miles from the old county town of Haverfordwest and its first-class shopping and other facilities.

Not surprisingly, Haverfordwest has increasingly become a major holiday base for visitors to the Dale Peninsula, Marloes Peninsula, St. Bride's Bay, and even the Preseli Hills. Indeed, Haverfordwest is ideally placed for exploring the whole of Pembrokeshire. It is only 16 miles from St. David's and Fishguard in the north, a similar distance from Whitland in the east, and just 11 and 19 miles respectively from Pembroke and Tenby in the south.

Even closer to Haverfordwest is the neighbouring town of Milford Haven and its new marina and dockside attractions. From here you can catch any of several pleasure boats which ply the Haven waterway to and from Skomer, Skokholm and Grassholm. These islands are vitally important habitats for a variety of birds and wildlife. Skomer and Skokholm are best known for their puffins, but they also support the world's largest population of Manx shearwaters. Grassholm has a similar claim to fame; its population of 33,000 pairs of gannets makes it the second largest gannetry in the Northern Hemisphere.

The waters along the coast here are of great environmental importance too. Around Skomer and the Marloes Peninsula is one of only two Marine Nature Reserves in Britain, and the warming influence of the Gulf Stream helps support a rare species of coral. Other marine inhabitants include dolphins, porpoise and Atlantic grey seals.

Another major natural attraction of the remote west is the Pembrokeshire Coastal Path, where walkers can discover the true meaning of solitude. There is a fascinating variety of landscape and geological features to be seen, and the broad sweep of St. Bride's Bay provides a magnificent coastal panorama.

In fact, wherever you choose to stay or by whichever means you choose to explore it, you will soon appreciate that the county's wild west coast presents you with yet a different face of the Pembrokeshire Coast National Park.

Haverfordwest

Distances: Fishguard 16, Milford Haven 7, Narberth 8, Pembroke 11, St. David' s 16, Tenby 19, Carmarthen 30 and London 245.

Haverfordwest, always more English than Welsh and the county town of Pembrokeshire is still the region's most important town, and the biggest centre for shopping and employment.

The town's name originated from its position at the lowest fording point of the Western Cleddau. 'Haverford' means 'the ford used by goats', the 'west' being added later to avoid confusion with the similarly-named towns of Hereford and Hertford.

Overlooking the town centre are the ruins of the medieval castle. The centre itself has a medieval street plan, but first appearances suggest that the only buildings older than late 18th century are the castle

Haverfordwest

and three Norman churches of St. Mary' s, St. Martin's and St. Thomas's. However, behind the new facades of many buildings are much older structures.

The castle was founded prior to 1120 and rebuilt in the 13th century, and only

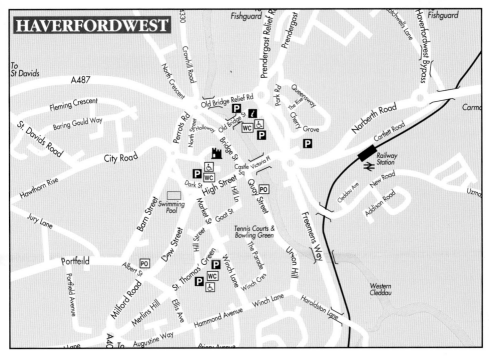

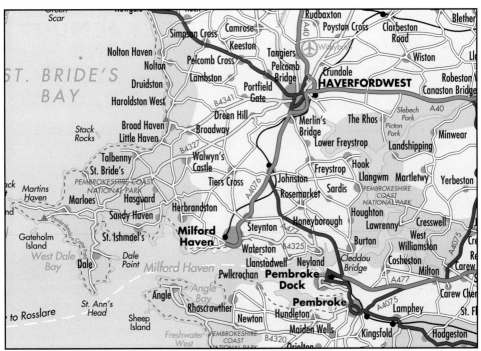

Pembroke was bigger. In 1220 the town was burnt at the hands of Llywelyn the Great, but the castle was undamaged. In 1405 Owain Glyndwr and more than 2,500 men put the town under siege, but again the castle proved impregnable. In the Civil War, Haverfordwest - like Pembroke and Tenby - was held in turn for both King and Parliament, before Cromwell ordered the castle to be slighted in 1648. He also decreed that Haverfordwest should become the county town in place of Pembroke. The keep and substantial sections of wall are all that remain of the castle today, though it has continued to serve the town well over the centuries. In the 18th and 19th centuries it was used as a gaol, until the new county gaol was built in 1820. It has also been a police station.

St. Mary's Church is one of South Wales' finest. Built in the 13th century but substantially altered in the 15th century, it has many outstanding features, including curved oak roofs, a brass dating back to 1651, and an early-English lancet window. St. Martin's, with its high steeple, is the town's oldest church and has undergone much restoration.

From Tudor times to the early part of this century, Haverfordwest was a flourishing port. Exports included wool, skins, corn, lime and coal, and among the imports were salt, iron, leather, finished goods, and French and Spanish wine. There was a regular if infrequent passenger service to London, which sailed once a month. From the 18th century, many small industries such as limekilns, boatyards, collieries and quarries sprang up alongside the Western Cleddau and further downstream. Large warehouses lined the quay in Haverfordwest, and the waterway was bustling with fleets of barges, coasting vessels and small steamships. But the decline of the port is a familiar story in 19th-century Wales. In 1853 the arrival of

THE PEMBROKESHIRE AGRICULTURAL SOCIETY

Pembrokeshire County Show

When the Pembrokeshire Agricultural Society put down its roots permanently on its magnificent Showground at Withybush in the year 1959, few could have foreseen the fantastic growth and development achieved by the County Show during the 40 years since.

The site at Withybush became available for purchase in 1974, and it was a wise and courageous decision by the leaders of the Society to take the plunge and secure the ownership of what has become the finest County Showground in Wales, if not in the whole of the UK.

The Society realised that this was the start of something big. The Show was growing and there was the scope for expansion and opportunities to occupy permanent buildings which today not only houses the various sections for the three days of the Show, but many other events and one day shows are held throughout the year.

Withybush has become the venue of the second best attended agricultural event in the whole of Wales, second only to the Royal Welsh. Attendances have continued to break records with crowds of 100,000 over the three days and with record numbers of livestock and trade stand exhibitions.

Primarily a shop window for agriculture the show also fulfils an educational role and is a thriving centre for business as well.

The 'object' of the Society is the "improvement and encouragement of agriculture" and the organisers' aim is to ensure that everyone going to the show, competitors and visitors, old and young alike, have a good time and enjoy themselves. It's this underlying theme of pleasure and enjoyment that has made the County Show such a popular attraction to the agricultural community and the large number of tourists that visit the County during the summer period. When **the Show opens on Tuesday, 15th August 2000,** visitors can expect to see some 3,800 animals, which includes the cream of Welsh livestock, many of which would have already paraded at the Royal Welsh and Royal England Shows. Avenues will be packed with tradestands displaying the finest and most up-to-date machinery.

The Show has special areas for forestry, conservation, the environment, outdoor pursuits, a huge flower and vegetable exhibition, craft section, and many stands for food, home cooking, bee keeping, poultry fanciers, to mention only a few of the vast array of interests that in essence comprise many small shows within the event.

Visitors to the County should not miss the opportunity of coming to the County Show which has something for everyone.

the first train in Haverfordwest was greeted with great celebration. Though this exciting event represented a milestone in the history of the South Wales Railway, it was also the kiss of death for the town's maritime trade. A new era in travel had dawned, and shipping could not compete.

Today, the once-hectic quay has become the Riverside Quay Shopping Centre. A modern and attractive development, it includes a large indoor market - a reminder that Haverfordwest has for centuries been an important market town. There is a wide range of fresh local produce on sale here, along with locally made crafts, and on Tuesday of every week the livestock mart comes to town. There is also a large open-air market held on Sundays on Withybush airfield.

Haverfordwest Town Museum: See page 150

Haverfordwest Sports Centre: See page 158

Bisley Munt: Located in the High Street, Bisley Munt is a stockist of beautiful and exclusive hand-finished Clogau Gold jewellery. The gold is mined in Snowdonia, which was once the location for Britain's largest and richest gold mine. Clogau Gold is said to be the purest and rarest in the world, and each piece of jewellery which contains it is made to very high standards and bears the Assay marks of Clogau St. David's and the Welsh Dragon. Wearers of Clogau Gold jewellery have included many members of the Royal Family. For further information ring 01437 763532.

Haverfordwest Priory: Robert Fitz-Tancred, castellan of Haverfordwest, who died in 1213, founded the Augustinian Priory of St. Mary & St. Thomas the

Martyr. In 1536, during Henry VIII's Dissolution of the Monasteries, it was stripped of its lead roof and the stonework was plundered. Not surprisingly it became a rich source of building stone, but at various times in later years also fulfilled other roles, such as a boatyard, smithy and stables. The ruins, within easy walking distance of the town centre, are now being excavated by a team of archaeologists working with CADW (Welsh Historic

PICTON CASTLE

Monuments), and many interesting finds have been made to date.

Picton Castle: Medieval Picton Castle, just south of Haverfordwest, is highly unusual in that it has remained occupied throughout its long history, and has been home to the same family for more than five centuries. The original castle was a Norman fortification of earth and timber, but it is thought that the present structure was built by Sir John Wogan, Justiciary of Ireland under Edward I. In 1405 the castle was captured and damaged by French mercenaries engaged in the revolt of Owain Glyndwr. In 1643, during the Civil War, the castle twice changed hands. First the Parliamentary garrison fell to the Royalist Earl of Carbery, but it was later recaptured by General Rowland Laugharne without military action, thereby avoiding any damage to the castle. Prior to this, in

the 15th century, Picton passed by marriage to the Philipps family, who are the present owners.

Today's visitors can enjoy the castle's magnificent grounds and attractions such as the garden shop, crafts shop, natural history exhibition, restaurant and tea rooms. There are also guided tours of the castle on selected days throughout the summer. For more information ring 01437 751326.

Scolton Heritage Park: Within the park's 60 acres of landscaped grounds and woodland stands Scolton House, which dates back to the 1840's and is furnished throughout in the style of the 1920's. New displays in the Victorian stable block illustrate what life was like on a Pembrokeshire country estate, including stabling, cart shed, carpenter's workshop and smithy. Other attractions include an

animal enclosure, arboretum, nature trail and a new 'green' Visitor Centre made entirely of local materials. For more information ring 01437 731328.

The Old Smithy, Simpson Cross: Acquired by Janet & Dario Algieri in early 1998, The Old Smithy at Simpson Cross is one of the oldest stone buildings in the area and was in a poor state of repair. After

Little Haven

renovation, it now boasts 2 well lit rooms full of genuine Welsh made crafts & giftware ranging from original paintings & prints by local artists, Welsh Royal Crystal, chocolate from the local Pembertons chocolate farm, toiletries from Caldey Island, Celtic stained glass plaques and much more.

There's a large car-park shared with the Pembrokeshire Motor Museum, and opposite is the Victorian Conservatory Tea Room making a combined visit to all three a pleasant outing. Seasonal opening plus weekends from mid November through to Christmas for the purchase of ideal local Christmas gifts. For more information ring: 01437 710628

The Rhos

Virtually on the doorstep of this quiet and attractive little village, situated about 2 miles to the south of the main A40 Haverfordwest-St. Clears road, is stately Picton Castle. The road through the village also gives you access to the banks of the Eastern Cleddau - an ideal picnic site on a warm summer's day. Facing you across the water here is the slipway at Landshipping, and a few hundred yards to your right is Picton Point - the confluence of the Western and Eastern Cleddau rivers.

Little Haven

This is a tiny village resort of great charm and beauty, nestling between high cliffs. The beach, a sandy cove which at low tide connects with neighbouring Broad Haven, is popular in summer with bathers and boaters. It is hard to imagine that coal from local pits was once exported from here. Welcoming inns, a restaurant and a pottery complement the appeal of this quaint old fishing village.

Nolton Haven

Scolton Manor

Broad Haven

A favourite beach for bathers since 1800, Broad Haven is the biggest and most popular resort on Pembrokeshire's west coast. Though it can hardly be described as over-developed, the village has good facilities, including guesthouses, a youth hostel, pubs, watersports equipment hire, and plenty of self-catering accommodation, from caravans to cottages. At the northern end of the superb long sandy beach are a number of interesting geological features - folding, stacks and natural arches. The Pembrokeshire Coast National Park Authority has a purpose-built information centre on the main car park, and organises guided walks and talks.

Newgale

A popular surfing resort, Newgale is a small village at the northeastern end of St. Bride's Bay, overlooking the impressive 2-mile stretch of Newgale Sands. The sands are separated from the road and village by a high ridge of pebbles. At exceptionally low tides the stumps of a drowned prehistoric forest are sometimes exposed.

Nolton Haven

This compact coastal village, with its attractive cove, is virtually midway between Little Haven and Newgale. In the 18th century coal was exported from here, and the line of the tramway which brought the anthracite and culm from the mines to the

Marloes

coast can still be seen. Standing alongside the old track bed is the Counting House, which recorded how many wagonloads of coal were transported to the quay. The quay itself, built in 1769, no longer exists. Half a mile north of Nolton Haven was Trefran Cliff Colliery, which worked coal seams beneath St. Bride's Bay between 1850 and 1905. Part of an old chimney and other ruins are now the only evidence of this once-thriving industry. The area around Nolton Haven, characterised by narrow lanes and bridle paths, is a popular location for pony trekking. About a mile inland is the village of Nolton. The bellcoted church of St. Madoc's has a medieval carved stone bracket.

Roch

Dominating the otherwise flat landscape for miles around, Roch Castle stands on an igneous rock outcrop. The origin of the castle and its large pele tower is unknown, but it is thought that it was built in the 13th century by Adam de Rupe. Legend says that he chose the site because of a prophecy that he would die from an adder's bite. Unluckily for him, an adder was brought into the castle in a bundle of firewood and duly fulfilled the prediction. Lucy Walter was born in the castle in 1630 and later became the mistress of Charles II, by whom she had a son - the ill-fated Duke of Monmouth, who was executed for rebellion against James II.

The small village of Roch has a 19th-century church with a circular churchyard. La Petite Maison, a restaurant with a licensed bar, boasts one of the best wine lists in Pembrokeshire and a huge choice of traditional Provencal dishes, or alternative dishes to suit your own taste.

Wolf's Castle

Wolf's Castle (also frequently referred to in print as Wolfscastle) is at the northern end of the Treffgarne Gorge, where in the early part of the century railwaymen toiled to blast an unlikely route through the very old and very hard rock bed in a bid to fulfil Brunel's dream. The motte and bailey castle stands near the centre of the village, which is popular with holidaymakers by virtue of its inn, hotel and pottery. Archaeological finds nearby include Roman tiles and slates, indicating the site of a fortified Romano-British villa.

The village was the birthplace in 1773 of Joseph Harris, who in 1814 published Seren Gomer - the first all-Welsh weekly newspaper.

Treffgarne

Approximately 6 miles north of Haverfordwest and 2 miles south of Wolf's Castle, Treffgarne was the birthplace (c1359) of the rebellious Welsh hero Owain Glyndwr. The village stands close to the wooded rocky gorge, through which runs the Western Cleddau river, railway line and main A40 trunk road. The Treffgarne Gorge was cut by meltwater rushing south towards Milford Haven during the retreat of the last Ice Age. The areas around the gorge are dotted with sites of early settlements and fortifications, and on the western side rises the igneous outcrop of Great Treffgarne Mountain and other striking rock formations.

Nolton Haven church

Nant-y-Coy Mill

Restored Nant-y-Coy Mill dates back to 1332 and possibly even earlier. The last corn was ground here in the 1950's, but the mill wheel is still turning - 150 years after it was built. The mill is a very attractive crafts centre, museum and tea room, with a nature trail leading up to Great Treffgarne Rocks, from where the views of the gorge are spectacular. You can also take a detour to Lion Rock and Bear Rock - two of the most distinctive features of the Pembrokeshire landscape.

The mill's very wide selection of quality craft products is displayed on two floors. There are examples of the finest Welsh wool and everything from pottery to prints. The presentation is made all the more interesting by the inclusion of items relating to local history. The tearoom has wheelchair access, as do the mill wheel and the first floor of the craft centre and museum. Nant-y-Coy Mill is open from Easter through till mid-October.

Rudbaxton

Rudbaxton is about 2 miles north of Haverfordwest and is the site of one of the region's most impressive earthworks - a motte and bailey fortress established in the 11th century. In a valley below the mound is the parish church of St. Michael. This dates from the 12th century and was restored in the 1870's.

Milford Haven

Distances: Fishguard 24, Haverfordwest 7, Narberth 15, Pembroke 7, St. David's 21, Tenby 17, Carmarthen 37 and London 253.

Since its development as a new town and whaling port in the late 18th century, Milford Haven has seen its economic fortunes seesaw. Sir William Hamilton, husband of Nelson's Emma, was granted permission to proceed with the development by an Act of Parliament of 1790. He appointed his nephew, Charles Francis Greville, to supervise the building of the town and port, and from the beginning it was envisaged that new Milford would secure its share of the transatlantic shipping trade.

Assisted by settlers from overseas - a group of American Quaker whalers from

Milford Haven

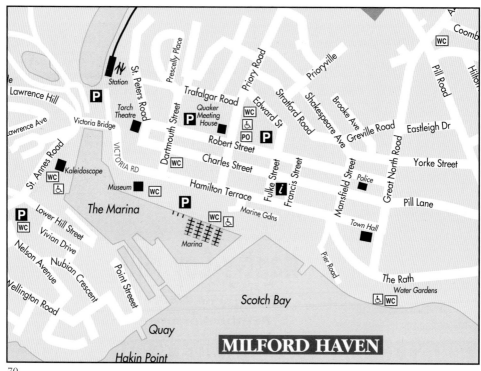

Nantucket and a Frenchman named Jean Louis Barrallier - Greville's progress was rapid, with the early establishment of a quay, custom house, inn and naval dockyard. When Nelson visited in 1802 both the new development and the Haven waterway, which he described as 'one of the world's finest natural harbours', suitably impressed him. The new inn was renamed 'The Lord Nelson' in honour of his visit; today it is a hotel, and a prominent building along Milford Haven's waterfront.

However, it was not long before the town's development suffered major setbacks. Greville died in 1809, whaling at the port ceased, and in 1814 the Admiralty transferred the naval dockyard several miles east to Paterchurch (now Pembroke Dock) - despite the fact that many fine ships had been built at Milford Haven in a very short space of time.

The Rath, Milford Haven

Another setback followed when, in 1836, the daily Irish Packet boat service was also moved from Milford to Paterchurch.

In the mid-1800's, a renewed effort was made to capture the transatlantic trade. Ambitious plans were drawn up for the building of docks to rival those of Liverpool and Southampton. Although these never materialised, the far more modest Milford Docks were opened in 1888, built in the inlet between Milford and Hakin.

The first vessel to enter the new docks was the steam trawler Sybil on 27th September 1888. Her arrival marked the beginning of a prosperous new era for Milford Haven as the port turned its attention to deep-sea fishing. The combination of new docks, excellent fishing grounds and good rail links saw the enterprise reap rich rewards.

Milford Haven thus became one of Britain's most successful fishing ports - an industry which was at its peak in the 1920's, when it employed 130 deep-sea trawlers and 4000 men afloat and ashore.

By the 1950's the seesaw had tipped the other way again as the fishing industry slipped into an irretrievable decline. This time, however, the promise of yet another new beginning for Milford Haven was already in the pipeline: the coming of the oil industry.

The oil companies were attracted to West Wales for a number of reasons. Of major consideration was the sheltered deep-water anchorage offered by the Haven waterway, which could accommodate crude oil tankers of ever-increasing size. The local authorities also made it clear they welcomed the new industry, pointing out the availability of a large labour pool.

A number of the world's best-known companies duly followed each other to Pembrokeshire. In 1960 the new Esso refinery was commissioned; in 1961 BP commissioned its ocean terminal at Angle Bay; in 1964 Regent Oil (now Texaco) brought its new refinery at Rhoscrowther into service; in 1968 Gulf opened its refinery at Waterston; and in 1973 Amoco (now Elf) commissioned a new refinery at Robeston. In a period of little more than a decade, Milford Haven was established as Britain's busiest - and Europe's biggest - oil port.

In recent years this industry too has had its ups and downs. The rising cost of crude oil in the 1970's and 1980's saw many refineries in Europe close, and a subsequent slimming down of the oil business around Milford Haven resulted in the closure of the Esso refinery in 1983 and the BP ocean terminal in 1985.

Only one refinery now remains, and despite the industry's problems the wealth generated by oil has helped fund Milford Haven's massive new investment in tourism. This has seen the complete refurbishment of the old docks and the creation of the superb 150-berth marina. Many old buildings have been demolished, while others of historic significance have been renovated and now house such attractions as the museum and Dockside Gallery. New buildings have sprung up too - notably that which is home to the fascinating Kaleidoscope Centre. The old shopping centre has been attractively remodelled, and the town's gardens and esplanade upgraded and landscaped to reflect their Victorian heritage. In addition, leisure facilities are first-class and the town's famous Torch Theatre provides a wide variety of entertainment on a scale to match many provincial big-city theatres.

Milford Marina: Since it so successfully hosted the start of the 1991 Cutty Sark Tall Ships Race, Milford

Welcome to
Milford Marina

Milford Marina is set in a non-tidal basin on the magnificent Milford Haven Waterway; the 22 miles of sheltered estuary offer all year round sailing. The amenity building provides a comprehensive range of facilities of a very high standard. There are boat repair facilities and storage available within the Docks, secure hard standing areas and an easy access slipway. Boat hoist and cranage facilities are also available.

- ▶ Easy access via M4
- ▶ London 4 hours
- ▶ British Rail station next to Docks
- ▶ Close to town centre
- ▶ Water & electricity to every berth
- ▶ Staff on duty 24 hours
- ▶ Member of the Yacht Harbour Association

MILFORD DOCKS,
MILFORD HAVEN,
PEMBROKESHIRE SA73 3AF
Tel: 01646 696312
Fax: 01646 696314
e-mail: marina@milford-docks.co.uk

ALL WEATHER ATTRACTIONS
KALEIDOSCOPE
INTERACTIVE DISCOVERY CENTRE
Working Fishing Boats • Boat Trips
• Historic Ships • Museum
• Golf Course • Dockside Gallery
• Adventure Playground
• Nature Trail

PIRATE PETE'S PLAY ADVENTURE
Fun and enjoyment for children 1-10yrs in a safe and stimulating environment

TEA ROOMS & RESTAURANTS
FREE PARKING

Marina has seen visitors returning in large numbers. The variety of attractions ensures there is something here for all ages, with go-karts, a superb dockside gallery, river cruises, the amazing Kaleidoscope Centre, Pirate Pete' s Play Adventure, quad bikes, miniboat rides, an adventure playground, nature trail, 9-hole golf course, pleasure boat trips, museum, and many other interesting sites and events. There is also an excellent variety of places to eat, to suit all tastes and budgets. The Dockside Diner is not just your ordinary fish and chip shop, and Martha' s Vineyard combines restaurant, lounge bar and tea rooms with superb views over the waterway. Then there' s the Sewin Restaurant and Waterfront Bistro, with a menu to delight every appetite. And wherever you choose to eat, you'll find that children are more than welcome. For more information about Milford Marina ring 01646 692272 (24 hr)

West River Club Cruises, Milford Marina: Milford Marina has many outstanding attractions, and West River Club Cruises is no exception. Comprising an American designed, 28 foot Bermudan sloop yacht, visitors can enjoy a unique perspective on Pembrokeshire - stunning marine life, dolphins and seals, offshore islands such as Skomer and Skokholm and beaches only accessible by boat. The trips that West River Club Cruises offer are suitable for all ages and can range from a relaxed family outing, to team building with work colleagues and even learning to take the helm yourself. With an RYA Approved Coastal Skipper on board, no experience is necessary! Alternatively, just sit back and enjoy the outstanding natural scenery that Pembrokeshire has to offer. On a fine day you can even take a swim from the anchored yacht or enjoy a barbecue on one of the splendid beaches. The yacht can hold a maximum party of six

and light refreshments are provided. To reserve a cruise call West River Club Cruises on 01646 698218. You can e-mail them on: the waltersgroup@milford marina.freeserve.co.uk or check out their website at: www.yachthire.co.uk

Kaleidoscope Discovery Centre, Milford Marina : This all weather magical indoor attraction is a very clever combination of puzzles, illusions and interactive games which educate and enthral by making science fun. Features include the amazing Kaleidosphere and many more electrifying and interactive exhibits. For more information ring 01646 695374.

Pirate Pete's Play Adventure, Milford Marina: Located in the foyer of the Kaleidoscope Centre, this fun attraction enables the under-10's to play in an exciting and safe environment while parents relax in the coffee shop opposite. The variety of ball pools, slides, swings and other features are guaranteed to keep youngsters occupied for hours on end. For more information ring 01646 695374.

Dockside Gallery, Milford Marina : The gallery, one of the finest in the county, is located in an old converted sail loft and shows a large and very impressive collection of arts and crafts created by Pembrokeshire craftspeople, artists and photographers. Displays are changed frequently, so there is always something new to see. For more information ring 01646 697702.

Milford Angling Supplies: The sea angling marks around and off the Pembrokeshire coast not only offer some of the best in Wales but can match the best in Britain. Shore venues include fine storm beaches, renowned for Bass and Flatties.

The Rath, Milford Haven

There are numerous rock ledges and walls from which Bull Huss, Conger, Dogfish, Garfish, Mackerel, Mullet, Pollack, Pouting and Wrasse are plentiful. Most are easily accessible and boat anglers are catered for by a variety of charter boats operating around the County. Small boat anglers who tow their own will find good launching facilities in many coastal and Cleddau/Milford Haven waterway towns. The boat angling can result in as many as 14 species on one trip. Best baits, for both shore and boat include fresh or frozen Mackerel, Squid, Sandeel and live

Ragworm. For the latest information on the "hot-spots" and other locations, together with all tackle and bait requirements why not call in to Milford Angling Supplies, The Docks, Milford Haven or phone 01646 692765, where the friendly staff will only be too pleased to help.

Milford Haven Museum, Milford Marina: Housed in the Old Custom House of 1797, this fascinating museum tells the story of Charles Francis Greville, who supervised the development of Milford into a new town and port two centuries ago, and of the American whalers from Nantucket who settled here. It also recalls the days in the port's history when trawlers and drifters filled the docks and 'every day was pay day', and relates Milford's role in two world wars and the arrival of the oil industry with its multi-million-pound refineries. For more information ring 01646 694496.

Torch Theatre: Milford Haven is fortunate to boast its own professional repertory theatre - one of only three in the whole of Wales. Built in the mid-seventies, it has a 300-seat auditorium and a resident production and touring company - the Torch Theatre Company - whose exciting and varied programmes over an 18-year period have attracted not only an ever-growing audience, but performers of the highest calibre.

The theatre has successfully set the stage for all kinds of entertainment - dance of every description, drama, music, children's theatre, comedy, light entertainment, and even top films and art exhibitions. The theatre is open all year round, and the Torch produce their own leaflet available from information centres which features the full programme. For tickets or more information ring 01646 695267.

Milford Haven Marina

Meads Sports & Leisure Centre, Milford Haven : See page 159

Neyland

A few miles east of Milford Haven is the small residential town of Neyland, which faces Pembroke Dock across the Haven waterway. At one time a ferry was the only link between the two, but since 1976 the Cleddau toll bridge has spanned the gap.

Like Milford Haven, Neyland has been revitalised by the building of an impressive new marina and waterfront development - Brunel Quay. Its name could only be a reference to the great railway engineer, whose aim was to establish Neyland as a prosperous transatlantic port by choosing it as the terminus of the South Wales Railway. (At one time or other during the 18th and 19th centuries, virtually every port and resort on the entire Welsh coast had designs on winning the battle for the highly lucrative transatlantic trade. Sadly, none of them ever succeeded.)

In the event, Neyland was not to realise this grand ambition, but until 1906 the town did become an important terminus for the Irish ferries. In that year

NEYLAND YACHT HAVEN
Wales's Premier Marina

The unrivalled position of the Marina provides the yachtsman with a superb location to explore the Pembrokeshire Coast National Park. 360 berths, access at all states of the tide, favourable rates, 24 hour security, fuel alongside, electricity, water, chandlery, showers, café, bar/restaurant etc. Please contact our Marina Staff who will be pleased to make any arrangements for your visit, or would be happy just to advise you.

Brunel Quay, Neyland, Pembrokeshire, SA73 1PY. Tel: (01646) 601 601 Fax: (01646) 600 713.

the service was transferred to Fishguard in the north of the county. But the railway remained operational until 1964, when the town's depot was closed.

The route of the old railway line now provides an enjoyable country walk between the new marina and the village of Rosemarket. Mountain bikers can also tackle the 14-mile circular Brunel Cycle Route. The 300-berth marina itself occupies the site where Brunel's depot and quay once stood, and in the last few years has established Neyland as a major sailing and watersports centre. Alongside the marina are attractive new homes and a popular waterside cafe. The redevelopment scheme has also created a fine promenade and picnic area, with superb views of the Cleddau Bridge and the busy waterway.

Neyland Yacht Haven : Neyland Yacht Haven is situated in a well-protected inlet adjacent to the town of Neyland some ten

Neyland Yacht Haven

Marloes Sands

miles from the entrance of the deep but sheltered waters of Milford Haven.

Since opening in 1985 this 380 berth marina's popularity has grown steadily. In fact with an unrivalled location and some of the finest facilities anywhere, it has established itself as the premier yachting centre in South West Wales.

The recent extended 24 hr access lower basin provides berthing for annual contract berth holders and visiting yachtsmen, whilst the more tranquil upper basin, above the half-tide cill, is favoured by our short-term berth holders and those visiting yachts who decide to extend their visit.

Whether exploring the offshore islands of the rugged Pembrokeshire coast, the quiet tree-lined creeks of this sheltered estuary, or enjoying the competition of the numerous racing events held by the local yacht clubs throughout the year, Neyland Yacht Haven makes the ideal base from which to enjoy these fascinating waters.

Llanstadwell

Llanstadwell

Just west of Neyland along the Haven shoreline, the small hillside village of Llanstadwell overlooks the estuary and Pembroke Dock, in the shadow of the former Gulf's Waterston refinery. There are some pretty cottages here, and the medieval parish church enjoys a picturesque position. The village inn and restaurant is a popular retreat.

St. Ishmael's

Located between Milford Haven and Dale, the village of St. Ishmael's lies in a deep sheltered valley. Nearby are important historic sites - a Norman motte and bailey to the north, and the Iron Age forts of Great and Little Castle Heads to the east. The 12th-century church stands away from the village, on the site where St. Ishmael is believed to have founded his principal church in the 6th century. A stream divides the churchyard.

Dale

The seaside village of Dale enjoys a sheltered position on the northern shoreline of the Haven waterway, close to the entrance at St. Ann's Head. It was here that Harri Tudor landed in 1485, after exile in France and marched overland to defeat Richard III at Bosworth Field and so become Henry VII.

This one-time shipbuilding and trading port is now one of the most popular sailing centres in Pembrokeshire, and has good facilities for visitors. Races are held on most days during the summer, and in August there is a regatta.

Close to the village is Dale Fort, one of the Victorian defences built to protect the waterway, and now used as a geographical field study centre. A footpath from the village takes you to the beautiful beach of West Dale Bay, which though dangerous for bathing faces southwest and is a real sun trap.

Dale

From the western end of Dale village, the road leads to the magnificent headland of St. Ann's Head, with its lighthouse and coastguard station. The history of the lighthouse dates back to the Middle Ages, when bonfires were lit on the cliffs to warn shipping of the perilous rocks around the headland. During winter months this very exposed peninsula is often blasted by winds of between 80 and 100 mph. But on a fine summer's day the views of the Haven waterway and its busy shipping lanes are breathtaking.

Marloes

This pretty little village with its attractive cottages and church lies en route to Marloes Sands, off the B4327. The church of St. Peter dates from the 13th century and was renovated in 1874. The village also has an interesting clock tower, given by Baron Kensington, who was owner of the nearby Deer Park estate. Marloes Sands can be reached from the village or from Dale. The panoramic views from the cliffs above the superb beach take in the islands of Skomer, Skokholm and the much smaller Gateholm, which at low tide can be reached from the northern end of the beach. The road through Marloes village also gives you access to the peaceful cove of Martin Haven - the departure point for Skomer Island and other island boat trips.

St David's & the North Coast

Compared with Tenby and the more developed south, North Pembrokeshire is better known for its rugged beauty and ancient landscape than for its leisure attractions and amusements. Yet many of the features which annually bring hundreds of thousands of visitors to the area can be described truthfully as man-made - some as long ago as 5000 years.

The sights awaiting those visitors with a will to explore are as fascinating as they are varied. They include such delights as the cathedral and city of St. David' s; the superb beach of Whitesands; the picturesque village and harbour of Solva; small coastal resorts such as Abereiddy and Porthgain; the golden sands of Newport; traditional crafts and Welsh industries such as working woollen mills; and the historic port of Fishguard. Inland, the beautiful Gwaun Valley and rolling Preseli Hills add their own mystique to a landscape liberally endowed with prehistoric sites and ancient burial chambers.

Reminders of earlier visitors can also be seen along North Pembrokeshire's magnificent coastline. During the Age of the Saints (400-800), and particularly in the 5th, 6th and 7th centuries, pioneering missionaries of the Celtic church braved the perils of the western seaboard to spread the gospel between Ireland, Wales, the Isle of Man, Cornwall and Brittany. These journeys on the high seas were fraught with danger, and as a mark of thanksgiving for their safe arrival on dry land they established chapels and shrines at the points of landing and departure. Consequently, Pembrokeshire's northern coast (and beyond into Cardiganshire) has a profusion of such churches and religious sites, each dedicated to a particular saint.

To the Welsh, the greatest saint of all was of course St. David - the patron saint of Wales. The spectacularly beautiful peninsula which bears his name is the most hallowed spot in the country, for this was his reputed birthplace. It was here that he established a semi-monastic religious settlement in around 550. This site is now occupied by the famous 12th-century cathedral which gives the village of St. David's its entitlement to city status. It is the smallest city in Britain; some sources claim it to be the smallest in the world.

St. David has given his name not only to the city and cathedral, but also to the peninsula which lies in the north western corner of Preseli Pembrokeshire. It is part of the National Park, and is often described as the Land's End of Wales since here you will find the most westerly point on the Welsh mainland. The peninsula is an undulating plateau 200 feet above sea level - a wild and windswept landscape with virtually no trees. The skyline is dominated not by the tower of St. David's Cathedral, as you might expect, but by stark hills of igneous rock such as Carn Llidi. If anything the cathedral is conspicuous by its absence, because until you are in its immediate vicinity it is very effectively hidden in the vale of the tiny River Alun.

Carn Llidi, close to St. David's Head, is deceptive to the eye. It rises a modest 600 feet above sea level, but looks much higher. It is certainly ancient; the rock of which it is made, called gabbro, is 500 million years old. In much more recent times, when sea

St David's Lifeboat Station

level was as much as 250 feet higher than it is today, Carn Llidi was an island in the Celtic Sea. Fortunately for today's visitors, it now stands firmly on dry land and the views from the top are fabulous. Laid out before you in spectacular fashion are the peninsula, the dramatic coastline and Ramsey Island; the 140-foot tower of South Bishop lighthouse several miles offshore is also easily distinguishable. On a clear day, you might even catch sight of the Wicklow Hills, 85 miles away on the Irish coast. It was because of the unprecedented views to the west and north that Carn Llidi proved strategically useful in both world wars. In the First it bore a hydrophone station for detecting submarines; in the Second it was the site for a lookout and radar installation.

The area around St. David's Head displays strong evidence of ancient settlements. Near the tip of the headland is a Neolithic burial chamber, Coetran Arthur, dating from about 3500 BC. This stands close to the site of an Iron Age settlement which was protected by a formidable defensive structure called Clawdd y Milwyr - Warriors' Dyke. Within the structure, which consisted of ramparts and ditches, are eight stone-lined hut circles. Nearby, on the slopes of Carn Llidi, are the remains of stone walls which formed part of an Iron Age field system.

South east of Carn Llidi, and overlooked by St. David's Head, is Whitesands Bay. This superb beach, very popular in summer, is the best in North Pembrokeshire and has been described as the best in Wales.

Whitesands is backed by The Burrows, an extensive area of sand dunes formed about 10,000 years ago and continually replenished as westerly winds whip up the sand on the beach and blow it inland. The dunes provide the perfect location for St. David's Golf Club. Unlike many other courses, the nine holes are playable all year round as water drains off quickly through the underlying sand. If you like playing your golf within 50 yards of a beach, this is the place to come, particularly as the club is always pleased to welcome visitors and new members.

South of Whitesands Bay is an expanse of countryside - an ancient agricultural landscape of fertile soils and arable fields. Further south still, the ruins of St. Justinian's Chapel stand near the little cove of Porthstinian, which is also the home of the St. David's Lifeboat Station. This was built in 1869.

Around the south western tip of the peninsula the cliff scenery is magnificent. To the east of Porthlysgi Bay and Porth Clais is St. Non's Bay, named after Non, the mother of St. David. This is where the patron saint is said to have been born, the exact spot marked by the ruins of St. Non's Chapel.

Fascinating it certainly is - and the St. David's Peninsula is only one of North Pembrokeshire's great attractions. As the following pages illustrate, there are many other treats in store for visitors who have the time and energy to seek them out.

St David's

Distances : Fishguard 16, Haverfordwest 16, Milford Haven 21, Narberth 25, Pembroke 26, Tenby 35, Carmarthen 46 and London 266.

St. David's is living proof that size is not important. As any visitor will quickly discover, the cathedral city is in reality a modest but very charming village. People still flock here in their thousands, as they did throughout the Middle Ages when this was a place of pilgrimage, and the

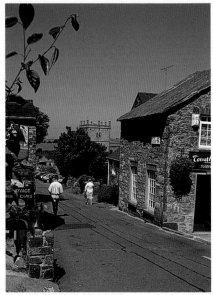
St David's

cathedral remains the major object of attention. Yet impressive and hugely significant though it is, the cathedral is small by English standards and because it is hidden in a sheltered valley you could pass through St. David's without even knowing that Wales' greatest religious monument is here.

The village-cum-city dates back to the 6th century and stands approximately a mile from the sea, on a wide plateau overlooking the diminutive River Alun. The centre of St. David's is marked by Cross Square, so called because of its restored ancient cross. High Street is something of a misnomer for the road which runs in from Solva and Haverfordwest, but it does contain City Hall.

Holiday attractions in St. David's include amongst others the Thousand Islands Expedition, (see page 136/137) but inevitably all roads lead to the 12th-century cathedral. Less well known, but no less impressive, are the ruins of the once-

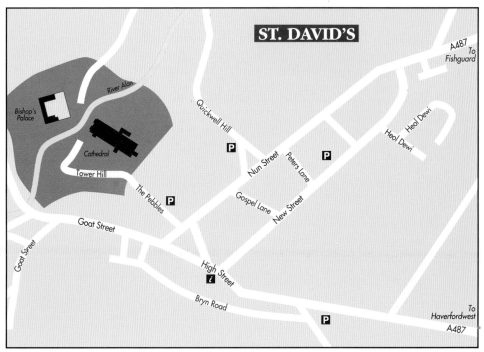

ST. DAVID'S

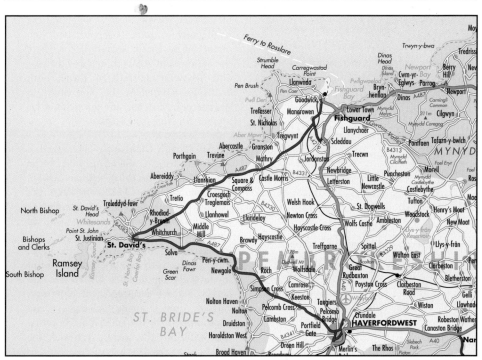

83

magnificent Bishop's Palace, which stand opposite the cathedral in Cathedral Close. The Close is an area of 18 acres, lying below the village in the vale of the River Alun. It is believed that this secluded site was chosen for the original 6th-century church so that it would not be visible from the sea to passing pirates and raiders, who frequently made it their business to ransack western coastal communities and pilfer whatever treasures the churches and chapels might contain. However, the ploy failed; Vikings burnt the church no less than eight times during the centuries leading up to the Norman Conquest.

The path from the village down to Cathedral Close takes you through the 13th-century Tower Gate - one of four gatehouses which formed part of the Close's precinct wall. Within the Close stands the cathedral, the Bishop's Palace and various other ecclesiastical buildings, including the houses of church dignitaries. At this point you are still above the level of the cathedral, and to reach it requires a further descent of a flight of thirty-nine steps (no connection with John Buchan) known as the Thirty-Nine Articles. The Cathedral and Bishop's Palace are marvels of medieval architecture, all the more striking for the remarkable tranquillity of this remote setting.

Very little is known of St. David himself. He was supposedly born just a short distance away, on the site of St. Non's Chapel to the south of the village, in the 6th century. The date given for his birth varies between 462, 500 and 530, while the legend that he died in 601 at the age of 147 puts the year of his birth at 453 or 454. Tradition has it that he died on 1st March 589, though such precision seems odd in the face of so much uncertainty. There is further confusion in the suggestion that the village of Llanon, south of Aberystwyth in neighbouring Cardiganshire, took its name from Non, mother of St. David, because this is where the patron saint was born in about the year 500. Whatever the truth, St. David's birth is commemorated by the Non Stone in Aberystwyth Museum, and the tomb of his mother, St. Non, is in Brittany.

St. David's Cathedral: The cathedral as it stands today was begun in 1180 by Peter de Leia, the third Norman bishop, and completed in 1522. In 1220 the central tower collapsed - an occurrence apparently not unknown in medieval churches - and further damage was inflicted by a severe earthquake in 1248. Early in the 14th century, Bishop Gower (nicknamed 'the building bishop' because of his love for creating great buildings) carried out many changes and improvements to the cathedral. He raised the walls of the aisles, inserted the

St David's Cathedral

decorated and much larger windows, built the south porch and transept chapels, and vaulted the Lady Chapel. In around 1340 he also built the Bishop's Palace to accommodate the large numbers of pilgrims visiting the cathedral. The palace, a structure of such splendour that even the ruins are impressive, stands opposite the cathedral.

As the cathedral expanded, an increasing number of clerical residences and other ecclesiastical buildings grew up around it, and a wall with gatehouses was built to protect the community. The last of the great builders to contribute to the cathedral was Bishop Vaughan, who in the early 16th century raised the tower to its present height and built the perpendicular chapel dedicated to the Holy Trinity.

Following the Reformation the cathedral was neglected. The roof of the Lady Chapel was stripped of its lead and subsequently - though much later - collapsed. Severe damage was also inflicted in the Civil War. In 1862 Sir George Gilbert Scott was commissioned to begin a complete restoration of the cathedral, and not surprisingly the work continued into this century. In 1866, during the restoration, the bones of two men were found in a recess which had been walled up. It is believed that these were the remains of St. David and his friend and teacher St. Justinian. They are now contained in an oak chest in the Holy Trinity chapel. Other tombs in the cathedral include those of Bishop Gower, Edmund Tudor - father of Henry VII - and Giraldus Cambrensis.

St. David's Cathedral, which is open to visitors every day, is the largest church in Wales, and certainly the most interesting. The total interior length is nearly 300 feet and the tower is 125 ft high: small by comparison with cathedrals on the grand scale of York Minster, but a mighty

St David's Cathedral

inspiration to the Welsh for centuries past and, no doubt, for centuries to come.

Bishop's Palace: This grand and richly decorated palace was largely the work of Bishop Henry de Gower, who also left his very distinctive mark on Lamphey Bishop's Palace and Swansea Castle. It was built mainly between 1328 and 1347, and stands opposite the cathedral in Cathedral Close, amongst a group of medieval buildings unique in Wales. The palace played host to many pilgrims, whose numbers included monks, bishops and kings. Even in ruin, the battlements, curtain walls, gatehouse and entrance to the Great Hall are impressive, and of particular interest are Bishop Gower's arcaded parapets, which are decorated with some of the finest examples of medieval sculptured heads and animals to be found in Wales.

choir school, St. David's still proudly boasts three outstanding choirs, whose presence will again bring great harmony to St. David's Cathedral Festival.

In 2000 this unique celebration of classical music takes place between 27th May and 4th June.

The Festival provides an excellent opportunity to combine a week's holiday in the beautiful Pembrokeshire Coast National Park with a feast of great music - and, of course, the chance to experience the most historic and revered building in Wales. For more information and booking details, ring the Festival Administrator on 01437 720271, or fax 01437 721885.

Thousand Island Expeditions, St. David's: See page 136/137

Ramsey Island Pleasure Cruises, St. Justinian's: For more information regarding Ramsey Island Pleasure Cruises please telephone 01437 721911.

The Bishop's Palace houses two fascinating exhibitions - Life in the Palace of a Prince of the Church and Lords of the Palace - it is also the venue for a number of special events. These include performances of Shakespeare plays and a December carol service. The palace is in the care of CADW (Welsh Historic Monuments) and is open every day except Christmas Eve, Christmas Day, Boxing Day and New Year's Day. For more information, including details of special events, ring 01437 720517 or 01222 465511.

St. David's Cathedral Festival: The Cathedral has a strong musical tradition going back to Thomas Tomkins, who was born here in 1572 and was a famous composer of his time. He was the son of the cathedral organist. The organ currently in use was built in 1883 by the great Henry Willis. It is one of the remarkable facts of Britain's smallest cathedral city that despite having a scant population and no

Nr Whitesands, St Davids

St. Non's Chapel, (St. Non's Bay)

Non was the mother of the man destined to become the patron saint of Wales. Standing in a field above St. Non's Bay, just south of St. David's, the original ruined chapel is reputedly the oldest Christian monument in Wales. It is also said to mark the exact spot where St. David was born in the 6th century, during a thunderstorm. Near the chapel is a holy well which miraculously appeared at the moment of birth. In the Middle Ages the well attracted many people who came to cure their ailments. The present St. Non's Chapel was built in 1934.

Porth Clais

In centuries past, this picturesque inlet was a busy little harbour - the port of the monastic community at St. David's. Its sheltered anchorage saw the comings and goings of countless monks, priests, pilgrims, Norman soldiers, pirates, and even kings. Purple stone from nearby Caerfai and Caerbwdy was landed here to

Porth Clais

help build the cathedral, along with Irish oak for the roof of the nave. According to the tales of The Mabinogion, this was where the great black boar from Ireland came ashore, pursued by King Arthur and his knights, who chased it over the Preseli Hills until the beast was finally slain in Cornwall.

The breakwater at Porth Clais is probably medieval, though it was rebuilt in the early 18th century. Trade thrived here in the Tudor and Stuart periods, with exports of cereal to the West Country. Later years saw the import of limestone to feed the four kilns on the quayside, two of which have been restored.

The Sloop Inn at Porthgain is probably one of the best-known pubs in the area. The pub dates back to 1743, when it was more a workers than walkers pub. Nowadays, the the Sloop Inn makes a welcome stop for those walking along the coastal path. The premises offer .good

Whitesands, St Davids

Solva

parking and space for children to play, and a large picnic area.

St. Justinian's

The name actually refers to the remains of St. Justinian's Chapel, but over time it has become synonymous with the little creek and harbour of Porthstinian. The presence of the chapel recalls the legend of St. Justinian, who founded a small religious community on nearby Ramsey Island. But the discipline he imposed on his followers was so strict that they rebelled and cut off his head, whereupon St. Justinian picked it up, walked over the sea to the mainland, laid down his head and died.

Porthstinian

Porthstinian is well known as the home of the St. David's lifeboat station. This was founded in 1868, though it was 1912 before the buildings and slipway were built. The rocky coastline and dangerous offshore reefs, such as the Smalls and the Bishops and Clerks, make this an extremely treacherous area for seaborne traffic, and the lifeboats which have seen service here have been involved in many dramatic rescues.

Porthstinian has a beach but is unsuitable for bathing. Just across the water is Ramsey Island, separated from the mainland by hazardous Ramsey Sound.

Solva

Without question this must be one of the most charming and attractive coastal villages in Britain. Just east of St. David's on the A487 Haverfordwest road, Solva is a beautiful rocky inlet which floods except at low tide, so providing a sheltered safe anchorage for yachts and pleasure craft.

Not surprisingly, this fine natural harbour has given the village a long seafaring tradition. Shipbuilding and maritime trade flourished here until the railway arrived in Pembrokeshire in the

Blue Lagoon

middle of the 19th century. In its heyday the busy port had a thriving import and export business, nine warehouses, twelve limekilns, a direct passenger service to New York, and also played an important role in the construction of the two remote lighthouses erected at different times on the Smalls - a treacherous cluster of jagged rocks lurking 21 miles off Pembrokeshire's west coast.

The facts relating to the passenger service to New York are a particularly fascinating slice of Solva's history. In 1848 the one-way fare for an adult (the service was aimed at emigrants) was £3. For this you were sure of a bed space but had to take your own food - and the voyage could take anything from 7 to 17 weeks!

The most popular part of this favourite holiday village, which is split into two, is Lower Solva, with its harbour, surviving limekilns and a charming selection of shops, pubs and restaurants. Shopping in Solva is a particularly surprising experience

for such a small place. The highlight is the large 'complex' created by combining four very traditional Welsh buildings into one - a quaint version of a city department store, offering a big choice of quality Welsh wool products and clothing, gifts, pottery, paintings, prints, books, confectionery and much more.

Solva is an excellent place to join the Pembrokeshire Coastal Path, as the cliff scenery on either side of the inlet is magnificent. If you just fancy an easy stroll you can walk along the harbour, or take the footpath above the opposite (eastern) side of the inlet. This takes you to the top of the Gribin - a strip of land between two valleys - where you can see the site of an Iron Age settlement and superb views of the village and harbour.

Middle Mill

Just north of Solva, a mile up the valley of the river of the same name, nestles the attractive little waterside hamlet of Middle

Mill. Here you will find a working woollen mill, which opened in 1907 and has been in production ever since. This family-run business invites you to watch the process that turns the finest Welsh wool into a range of high-quality rugs, tweeds, carpets and clothes, all of which are for sale on the premises.

Abercastle

Abercastle stands on Pembrokeshire's rocky northern coastline, southwest of Strumble Head and close to the villages of Trevine and Mathry. From the 16th century on this was a busy little coastal port, at various times in its history involved in the export of corn, butter and oats and the import of general goods, anthracite, culm and limestone. The limekiln still survives on the attractive harbour. Abercastle can claim a small piece of important maritime history: in 1876 the first man to sail solo across the Atlantic landed here.

Abercastle

Llanrhian Church

Half a mile west of the village, standing just off the coast path, is Carreg Samson - an excellent example of a Bronze Age burial chamber. The capstone is 15 feet long and 9 feet wide, and according to legend Samson placed it in position using only his little finger.

Abereiddy

An attractive west-facing bay on the north coast of the St. David's Peninsula, Abereiddy is famous locally for its striking Blue Lagoon - once a slate quarry linked to the sea by a narrow channel but closed in 1904 after it was flooded during a storm. The lagoon is now considered an important geological feature, and the quarry yields many fossils. The coastal scenery between here and St. David's Head is outstanding. To the north there are traces of the old narrow-gauge railway track which once took the quarried slate and shale to the harbour at nearby Porthgain for export.

Abereiddy is about two miles east of Croesgoch, on the A487 St. David's-Fishguard road.

Llanrhian

Llanrhianis a hamlet standing at a crossroads on the road between Croesgoch

THE SLOOP INN 1743 AD

Porthgain ~ on the Pembrokeshire Coastal Path

The Sloop Inn, probably the best known pub in the county, is situated just 100 yards from the harbour of Porthgain. Relics and old photographs adorn the walls and ceilings, which makes it as much a museum as a pub. The menu is varied, catering for all tastes including vegetarians and children. Bar meals are available for lunch 12.00 - 2.30 p.m and a full menu is available in the evenings 6.00 - 9.30 pm. every day.

The Sloop Inn overlooks the village green where the kids can play and there is ample parking.

TELEPHONE: 01348 831449

and Porthgain. It is notable because of the unusual parish church, dedicated to St. Rheian, which is cruciform in shape and has a number of interesting features including a 15th-century ten-sided font. Also striking is the tall tower, built in the 13th century. The rest of the church was completely rebuilt in 1836 and restored in 1891.

Porthgain

A small hamlet in the parish of Llanrhian, Porthgain is one of the most individual places in Pembrokeshire, with superb coastal scenery, an unpretentious mixture of traditional, Victorian and later style houses, and a man-made, 19th Century harbour. The harbour at little Porthgain was then a hive of activity and its reconstruction between 1902 and 1904 to make way for larger quays reflected its significant shipping activities. These included the exportation of slate and shale from the quarry at Abereiddy and bricks

made from local clay, used mainly for local use. The main export however was the medium to fine granite stone; exceptionally hard and used for the construction of buildings and roads as far apart as Liverpool, Dublin and London. Porthgain was a village whose employment was entirely dependent on the prosperity of the quarry and by the turn of the century, the company known as 'Porthgain Village Industries Ltd' boasted a fleet of nearly 100 vessels including six steam coasters of 350 tons each. Even as late as 1931, the harbour was improved for a hoped for 170 ft 650 ton ship to enter, but after the First World War this maritime trade went into decline, as it did all over Britain due to the Slump, and by 1931 had ceased production entirely. In 1983 the Pembrokeshire Coast National Park Authority acquired the attractive harbour and the remains of the

Porthgain

buildings which bear testimony to Porthgain's industrial past.

Porthgain remains a very living community with a flourishing tourist trade due to it's magnificent stretch of coastline and many significant antiquarian remains, making it a must see for those interested in either industrial archaeology or ancient history. The Neolithic standing stones known as Carreg Samson near Abercastle date back as early as 3000 BC and a couple of miles north-east of Porthgain lies a fine Iron Age fort called Castell Coch. Porthgain is well worth a visit for its diversity of interest. One of Britain's finest geographers described the coast between Porthgain and Abereiddi as the finest in Britain and, as well as having a good sandy beach at the harbour, it is home to the 'The Sloop Inn' - probably the best known pub in the county.

Trevine

Just to the east of Porthgain and its attractive harbour, Trevine is the largest coastal village between St. David's and Fishguard. It is close to a shingle and sand beach known as Aber Felin, and the proximity of the coast path makes this a popular watering hole for walkers. There is also a youth hostel in the village. Near the shoreline stands the ruin of Trefin Mill, which closed in 1918 and has been partly restored by the National Park Authority. The mill was immortalised in the famous Welsh poem Melin Trefin - the name given to the village's newest attraction. Melin Trefin (described below) is a handweaving centre, craft shop and tearooms which opened in 1993.

Mathry

The village of Mathry stands on a hill just off the A487 between St. David's and Fishguard, a few miles east of Trevine. Its elevated position gives superb coastal

views, and of particular interest here is the parish church. This unusual squat building and circular churchyard occupy a prehistoric site, possibly dating from the Iron Age. At one time the church had a steeple that served as a landmark for mariners. Like Trevine, the village is a popular watering hole for visitors passing through. Just west of Mathry is the site of an ancient burial chamber.

View from Carnllidi, Nr St Davids

Goodwick

Until the harbour was completed in 1906, Goodwick was nothing more than a cluster of fishermen's cottages. But as the new terminus for the main railway line from London, this one-time village quickly adopted the status of a major ferry port and today is still the link between Fishguard and Rosslare in Ireland. This role became even more significant in 1994 with the introduction of the new high-speed SeaLynx service, which has reduced crossing times to as little as 99 minutes! Inevitably, Goodwick has grown so close, in every sense, to its very near neighbour Fishguard that it is now virtually a suburb of the larger town and the two are synonymous.

Letterston

Something's Cooking: This Award Winning, Family Run, Licensed Restaurant and Take Away serves some of the best fish and chips in the United Kingdom – and that's official!

In tradition with it's past quality awards and continual pursuit of excellence, Something's Cooking recently received the title of national winner in the 1999 *Fish and Chip Shop* of the year Competition and named 'Best fish and chip shop in Wales.' It doesn't stop there though. The adjoining restaurant offers morning coffee, Lunchtime Specials, Evening Meals, Children's menu and a variety of seafood in very pleasant surroundings. Draught beers, wine and spirits are also available.

So why not enjoy one of Britain's greatest traditions – at one of its greatest establishments. Open all day, Monday to Saturday 10am – 10.30 pm (including Bank Holidays) Sundays 6pm-10pm

View from Garn Fawr

Fishguard

Distances: Haverfordwest 16, Milford Haven 22, Narberth 24, Pembroke 26, Tenby 35, Carmarthen 46 and London 272.

Fishguard and Goodwick, 16 miles northeast of St. David's, are the only parts of Pembrokeshire's outer coastline which are not within the National Park. But they are certainly no less attractive for that, offering a good choice of accommodation and an ideal base for discovering all that this part of the county has to show you.

The harbour is in fact the main sailing centre of the North Pembrokeshire coast. Before the harbour was built, Fishguard had established itself as a very busy port, with slate, corn, butter and cured pilchards and herrings representing the main exports. During the 18th century only Haverfordwest was handling a greater volume of trade. Shipbuilding was important too; the shipyard was renowned for its schooners and square-rigged vessels.

The harbour and impressive breakwater on the Goodwick side of the bay were built in 1906 to attract the transatlantic liners away from Liverpool and Southampton. But as was the reality for Milford Haven, Cardigan, New Quay and other hopeful West Wales ports, the big dream did not materialise. However, there was compensation in successfully establishing the ferry links with Ireland - a lasting and positive return on the massive task of constructing the breakwater, which consumed 800 tons of rock along every foot of its half-mile length!

Fishguard has remained a major British ferry port, its status enhanced by the high-speed SeaLynx and excellent new port facilities. However, Fishguard's biggest contribution to the history books occurred

Lower Fishguard

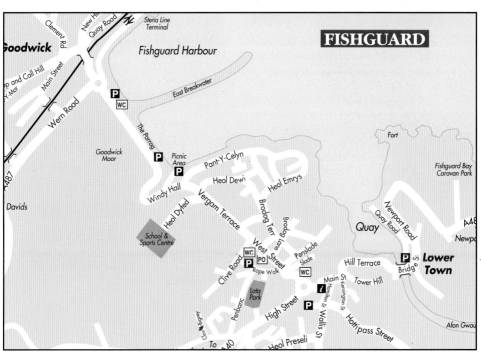

FISHGUARD

Goodwick

Fishguard Harbour

Stena Line Terminal

East Breakwater

The Parrog

Goodwick Moor

Picnic Area

Pant-Y-Celyn

Heol Dewi

Heol Emrys

Windy Hall

Heol Dyfed

Vergam Terrace

Brodog Terr

Brodog Lane

Fort

Fishguard Bay Caravan Park

Newport Road
Quay Road

Quay

Newpo

Lower Town

Davids

School & Sports Centre

Clive Road

West Street

PO

Rope Walk

Penslade
Slade

Hill Terrace

Tower Hill

Bridge St

Penbanc

Lota Park

High Street

Main St

Kensington St

Wallis St

Hamilton St

Hott pass Street

Afon Gwau

To A40

Heol Preseli

Clos Bryngwyn

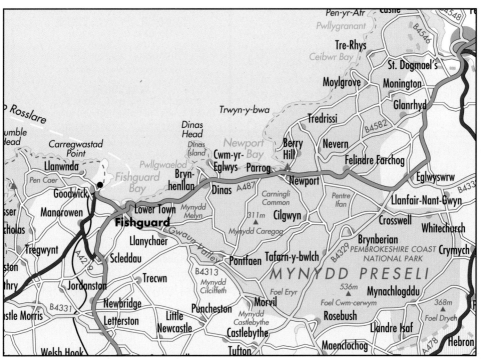

Pen-yr-Afr

Pwllgranant

Tre-Rhys

Ceibwr Bay

St. Dogmael's

Moylgrove

Monington

Glanrhyd

Rosslare

umble
ead

Carregwastad Point

Llanwnda

Pen Caer

Fishguard Bay

Dinas Head

Dinas
(Island)

Pwllgwaelod

Bryn-
henllan

Trwyn-y-bwa

Newport Bay

Cwm-yr-
Eglwys

Parrog

Tredrissi

Berry Hill

Nevern

Felindre Farchog

Eglwyswrw

Goodwick

Manorowen

Lower Town

Fishguard

Dinas

A487

Newport

Carningli Common

Pentre Ifan

Llanfair-Nant-Gwyn

Mynydd Melyn

Mynydd Caregog

311m

Cilgwyn

Crosswell

Whitechurch

sser

cholas

thry

ston

Tregwynt

Jordanston

Llanychaer

Scleddau

Trecwn

B4313

Gwaun Valley

Pontfaen

Tafarn-y-bwlch

Brynberian

PEMBROKESHIRE COAST
NATIONAL PARK

Crymych

MYNYDD PRESELI

Mynydd Cilciffeth

Foel Eryr

536m

Foel Cwm-cerwym

Mynachlogddu

368m

Foel Drych

stle Morris

Welsh Hook

Newbridge

Letterston

Little Newcastle

Puncheston

Castlebythe

Mynydd Castlebythe

Tufton

Morvil

Rosebush

Llandre Isaf

Maenclochog

Hebron

on 22nd February 1797, when the town was the scene of an extraordinary invasion which has the distinction of being the last invasion of British soil.

The uninvited guests were members of a French expeditionary force under the command of an American-Irish adventurer, Colonel William Tate, who had a commission in the French army. His mission was to seize Bristol - at that time Britain's second city - but bad weather forced the ships to land at Carreg Wastad Point, northwest of Fishguard. Once ashore, Tate's troops set about pilfering farms and homesteads, gorging themselves with as much food as they could lay their hands on, washed down with barrels of spirit which the local people had salvaged from a recent shipwreck. In this somewhat unfit condition the soldiers approached the town and, according to local tradition, mistook a crowd of women in red shawls and tall hats for guardsmen. The leader of these women, Jemima Nicholas, a Fishguard cobbler-woman, is said to have captured a dozen Frenchmen single handed, armed only with a pitchfork! Her heroism is remembered in the form of a monument in the churchyard at St. Mary's, where she is buried. Within 48 hours of landing, the French had surrendered.

Modern-day Fishguard is split into two distinct parts. The busy upper part is much like any small town, with many shops, pubs and places to eat. The Lower Town is much older and very attractive, its pretty cottages clustered around the old harbour, where the River Gwaun reaches the sea. In 1971 Lower Fishguard temporarily changed its identity to the fictional town of Llareggub when this picturesque location was chosen for the film version of Dylan Thomas's famous radio play 'Under Milk Wood', and was also the location for the making of the Orson Welles classic Moby Dick.

The landscape around Fishguard is truly magnificent. To the northwest is dramatic Strumble Head, where the lighthouse is linked to the cliff by a causeway. Dinas Head dominates the coast to the northeast, while to the south-east is the beautiful wooded Gwaun Valley. The whole area is dotted with prehistoric sites.

Last Invasion Embroidered Tapestry, Fishguard: Fishguard, 1797 and the French army, led by the American General

31st FISHGUARD INTERNATIONAL MUSIC FESTIVAL
21-29 JULY 2000

BBC National Orchestra of Wales (Tadaaki Otaka)
Tallis Scholars (Peter Phillips)
Pembrokeshire Youth Choir (John S. Davies)
Running Wild (jazz tribute to Goodman, Krupa, Hampton)
Fibonacci Sequence • Harfenspieler • London Winds
Skampa String Quartet • James Clark (in residence)
Nicolai Demidenko • John Suchet.
Poetry, children's and "Live music Now" events etc.

Details (all year round)
Festival Office, Fishguard, Pembs SA65 9BJ
tel/fax. 01348-873612
email: fishguard-imf@cwcom.net

The Last Invasion Tapestry

Tate are defeated. Jemima Nicholas, now a larger than life local heroine, contributed to this defeat.

That was the last invasion of British soil and all of the events can now be recalled in Elizabeth Cramp's vivid and carefully researched tapestry. 30 metres (100ft) in length and superbly characterised with life and humour; cows cavorting, dogs fleeing, soldiers, ships, flags, the rugged Pembrokeshire coastline and the still existing buildings such as Llanwnda Church and the Royal Oak Inn can be seen. It's all there - Don't miss it.

Melin Tregwynt Woollen Mill, Abermawr, Fishguard: For more information ring 01348 891225

Llangloffan Farmhouse Cheese Centre, near Fishguard : Llangloffan Farmhouse Cheeses are sold in outlets far and wide, including the famous Zingerman's Delicatessen in New York.

The Gwaun Valley

The Gwaun Valley is exceptionally beautiful and runs inland from Lower Fishguard to its source high on the slopes of Foel Eryr in the Preseli Hills. It is one of several inland areas of Pembrokeshire which fall within the National Park, and is regarded by geologists as the best example in the British Isles, if not the world, of a sub-glacial meltwater channel.

What this means is that about 200,000 years ago, towards the end of one of several recurring Ice Ages which have gripped the planet, the climate became progressively warmer and water began to tunnel beneath the melting ice. This meltwater was under intense pressure, the ice acting as a sort of geological pipe, and it moved with such tremendous force that it flowed uphill for long stretches. As this unstoppable water eventually crashed down towards the sea, taking with it huge boulders and blocks of ice, it created deep, steep-sided gorges in the landscape. Such are the awesome forces of nature which have given us the spectacular Gwaun Valley.

The valley is narrow and sheltered, with heavily wooded sides stretching up to 200 feet high. It is rich in wildlife and prehistoric remains, with an abundance of wild flowers and such birds as the buzzard, kestrel, owl, kingfisher, warbler and dipper. The River Gwaun, low and gentle in the summer, becomes a roaring torrent in winter as it rushes down from the Preseli Hills rising behind the valley.

Most of the valley's small communities are centred around the hamlets of Llanychaer and Pontfaen. These are largely farming communities, as much of the valley floor is farmed, and several farmhouses boast interesting architectural

Gwaun Valley

features such as distinctive Flemish-style chimneys.

The people of the valley are distinctive too; not in appearance, but in the fact that they are sticklers for local tradition. They still celebrate New Year's Day on 13th January according to the old Gregorian calendar - despite the fact that the change to the Julian calendar was made legal in 1752!

The Gwaun Valley and neighbouring Preseli Hills are well endowed with standing stones. For example, near Llanychaer you will find - with a little patience - the longest megalithic alignment in Wales. It is called Parc y Meirw (Field of the Dead), and is about 130 feet long. Four of its eight stone pillars are still standing, but its presence is not obvious at first sight because some of the stones are embedded in a hedgebank.

Other interesting stones can be seen at the restored church in picturesque Pontfaen, where memorial stones dating from the 9th century stand in the churchyard.

The ancient woodland of the Gwaun Valley is very precious, and parts of it have been designated as SSSI's - Sites of Special Scientific Interest. The species to be found here include oak, ash, sycamore, alder, blackthorn, hazel, hornbeam, wild cherry and wych elm, and the National Park Authority has established the Cilrhedyn Woodland Centre to promote good woodland management in the valley. Though very much a working centre for the Park Authority's woodland experts and rangers, it is planned to encourage visitors to the centre on a limited number of special open days during the main holiday season. More details of this can be obtained from any National Park Information Centre.

The National Park Authority has also made the valley more accessible on foot by

creating the Golden Road Path. This takes you from Lower Fishguard to Crymych via the ridge of the Preseli Hills, passing such fascinating features as Bronze Age burial mounds, a Neolithic burial chamber, a particularly fine example of an Iron Age fort, and Carn Meini - the source of the bluestone which thousands of years ago mysteriously found its way to Stonehenge for the construction of the monument's inner circle.

Newport

Newport is a very popular resort. The charming little town sits on the lower slopes of Carn Ingli, which rises to more than 1100 feet above sea level, and the superb stretch of sands on the east side of the Nevern estuary is rivalled only by Whitesands Bay as the best beach in North Pembrokeshire.

On the opposite shore of the estuary mouth is Parrog. It was here that Newport developed as a thriving port engaged in fishing, coastal trading and shipbuilding. Herrings were exported to Ireland, France and Spain, and by 1566 Newport was an important wool centre. However, this industry faltered when an outbreak of plague hit the town during the reign of Elizabeth I and much business was lost to Fishguard. Later in the port's development, slates quarried from local cliffs went by sea to Haverfordwest, Pembroke, Tenby and parts of Ireland. In 1825 maritime trade received a boost when the quay was built, and come the end of the 19th century Newport boasted five warehouses, several limekilns, coal yards and a successful shipyard. But today the estuary is silted up and it is pleasure craft that occupy the moorings.

As for the town itself, one of the main features is Newport Castle. This overlooks the estuary and was built in the early 13th century by William FitzMartin. It has had

Newport

an eventful history: captured by Llywelyn the Great in 1215, then by Llywelyn the Last in 1257, and attacked and damaged in Owain Glyndwr's revolt in 1408, after which it fell into decline. It remained a ruin until 1859, when the gatehouse and one of its towers were converted into a residence. Today the castle is in private ownership and not open to visitors. You can, however, see William FitzMartin's other contribution to Newport. He established St. Mary's, a huge church which is cruciform in plan and features a 13th-century Norman tower.

Other attractions in Newport include a 9-hole golf course alongside the sands, and the prehistoric cromlech known as Carreg Goetan Arthur, which stands in a field by the bridge. There are many such sites in the area. On Carn Ingli Common there are prehistoric hut circles and stones, and the most striking and famous site of all is Pentre Ifan, 3 miles southeast of Newport. This Neolithic chambered tomb is one of

Nevern Church

the finest in Britain, with 3 upright stones over 6 feet high supporting a huge capstone.

Nevern

Nevern is an ancient parish on the River Nyfer, close to Newport. Its imposing Norman church, dedicated to the Celtic saint Brynach, has a definite mystique and atmosphere that is compounded by the famous bleeding yew in the churchyard - a broken branch that constantly drips blood-red sap. The church is late perpendicular in style and features a magnificent 11th-century wheel-headed Celtic cross. This stands 13 feet high and rivals the cross at Carew. In and around the church are 4 more early Christian monuments, including the Vitalianus Stone. Above the church, topping a deep ravine, is Nevern Castle - a motte and bailey earthwork.

Moylegrove

This attractive coastal village stands on the Newport-St. Dogmael's road, a mile from Ceibwr Bay. It dates back to Norman times and nearby are two burial chambers. Small cargo ships once used the bay, and high cliffs and secluded coves marks the coast here, where Atlantic grey seals often bask.

St. Dogmael's

Facing Cardigan across the Teifi estuary is the picturesque hillside village of St. Dogmael's. It lies close to Poppit Sands, the most northerly beach in the National Park and also the northern end of the Pembrokeshire Coastal Path.

In St. Dogmael's you will find the remains of a 12th-century abbey. It was built in 1115 by Benedictine monks from France - a replacement for an earlier Celtic monastery which had stood on the site until Viking raiders destroyed it in the 10th

Ceibwr Bay

century. The north and west walls of the nave are still standing. Next to the abbey ruins is the parish church of St. Thomas the Martyr. It contains the Sagranus Stone, which bears an inscription that proved to be the key in deciphering the ancient Ogham script in 1848.

Cilgerran

Famous for its superb Norman castle, which is perched above the wooded gorge of the Teifi, Cilgerran is a few miles east of Cardigan and was once a slate quarrymen's village. It is the venue for the annual coracle regatta, which takes place in August.

The Teifi estuary

The River Teifi is a natural boundary between Pembrokeshire and Cardiganshire, and its wide estuary is of great interest. The large and popular beach of Poppit Sands is backed by extensive dunes and has good visitor facilities. The area is also

excellent walking and watersports country, and the estuary is a favourite haunt for birdwatchers. The many species to be observed here include gulls, oystercatchers, curlews, cormorants and shelduck. The Teifi is also well known for its salmon and sea trout, and the ancient Teifi coracle was used by fishermen long before the Romans arrived.

The valley of the Teifi, which a little further inland separates the counties of Cardiganshire and Carmarthenshire, is said to be one of the most beautiful river valleys in Britain. It is certainly very scenic, with several picturesque towns and villages along its banks, and for visitors to North Pembrokeshire is well worth exploring.

The West Wales ECO Centre, Newport: The West Wales ECO centre is Pembrokeshire's premier energy and environment attraction. For more information ring 01239 820235

The Preseli Hills

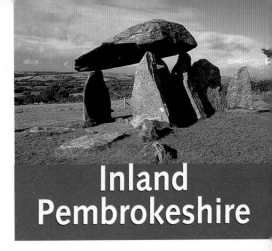

In the ancient Welsh tales of The Mabinogion, Pembrokeshire was described as 'Gwlad hud a lledrith' - the land of magic and enchantment. And nowhere is this magic and enchantment more evident than in the wild, mysterious Preseli Hills.

These rolling moorlands, often overlooked by visitors on their way to the coast, are the major upland region of the National Park, presenting a stark contrast to the relatively flat coastal plateau. The hills do not aspire to any great height - the highest summit, Foel Cwm Cerwyn, is 1760 feet above sea level - but the many remains of hillforts, burial chambers and other monuments are proof that even prehistoric man had a powerful affinity with this bleak and mystical landscape.

The evidence left by the earliest settlers suggests man has occupied the hills for at least 5000 years. Neolithic burial chambers, Bronze Age cairns, stone circles, standing stones and Iron Age forts litter this untouched Celtic landscape.

When Neolithic (New Stone Age) farmers arrived in Pembrokeshire, well versed in the art of raising crops and herding animals, they were the first people to work the land here. They fashioned implements such as axes, hammers and hoes from Preseli dolerite (bluestone), and archaeologists believe that two so-called 'axe factories' existed on the Preseli Hills, though their sites have never been identified.

The dwellings of these distant ancestors were too flimsy to stand up to the ravages of time. But not so their tombs (cromlechau), which are concentrated along the coastal plateau and in the Preseli foothills. Pentre Ifan, on the hills' northern slopes, and Carreg Samson, on the coast near Abercastle, are two of the finest prehistoric monuments to be found anywhere in Wales.

Later Bronze Age man also left his burial sites on the Preseli Hills, in the form of round cairns. A fine example is that to be found on top of Foel Drygarn. There is another on the summit of Foel Cwm Cerwyn, the highest point in all Pembrokeshire. On exceptionally clear days the views from here are astonishing. You can see west to the Wicklow Mountains of Ireland, north to Snowdonia, east to the Brecon Beacons and south across the Bristol Channel to the counties of the West Country.

Another ancient relic adorning the Preseli Hills is the interesting stone circle known as Gors Fawr. This stands on the moorland west of the hamlet of Mynachlogddu. It comprises 16 stones and 2 large outlying pointer stones, and its diameter exceeds 70 feet.

Quiet roads in the Preseli Hills

Preseli Hills

But the biggest mystery of all to emanate from these brooding hills - and one which seems unlikely ever to be answered - concerns the inner circle at Stonehenge, 180 miles from Preseli on Salisbury Plain. Much of this inner circle is made from bluestone, which is dolerite, rhyolite and volcanic ash, found only at Carn Meini on the eastern crests of the Preseli Hills. The mystery is how the 80 stones, weighing up to 4 tons each and over 250 tons in total, made the incredible journey from Preseli to Salisbury Plain during the third millennium BC.

The most likely explanation seems to be that they were taken by boat along rivers and up the Bristol Channel, crossing the overland stretches on sledges which had rollers underneath. This would have taken a gargantuan effort by a huge army of labour. Even so, this theory has found much wider acceptance than the two others proposed.

One is that the stones were carried to Salisbury Plain by the great Irish Sea Glacier - the biggest flow of glacial ice ever to cover Britain - long before the builders of Stonehenge set about their task. But even many geologists doubt that this is the case.

The other suggestion, and by far the most fanciful, is that levitation is the answer. It is proposed that the builders of Stonehenge had mystical powers and could magically raise stones off the ground merely by thinking about it. Other stories from around the world tell of stones being moved in this way.

The Preseli Hills have inspired other myths and legends. Predictably, King Arthur has strong associations here. A tale from The Mabinogion tells how he pursued a great black boar across these hills from Ireland, and his name is remembered in such places as Carn Arthur.

Exploring the Preseli Hills won't bring you into contact with the legendary black boar, but there are certainly other creatures of interest to see. Wild ponies still roam free on the hills, and among the birds which frequent this upland territory are kestrels, meadow pipits, skylarks and wheatears.

There are also plenty of places of interest to discover in and around Preseli and its foothills. The little village of Rosebush, for example, lies in the shadow of Foel Cwm Cerwyn. It is notable for its slate quarries and for its ambitious though failed plans to take advantage of the arrival of the railway in the 19th century and become a tourist resort. Just southwest of Rosebush is the beautiful Llysyfran Reservoir and Country Park, which has many attractions for visitors.

In the north, the hills sweep down to the sea between Newport and Fishguard. Carn Ingli, overlooking Newport Bay and the rocky promontory of Dinas Head, is the nearest Preseli summit to the sea, cut off from the main range by the extremely picturesque Gwaun Valley. Close to the resort town of Newport are such delights as Nevern, with its haunting church, and the reconstructed Iron Age hillfort at Castell Henllys. A little further north are the dramatic cliffs of Cemaes Head, where the exposed rocks have been folded by the tremendous forces exerted by movements deep in the earth. The cliffs of the headland are over 500 feet high in places - the highest in Pembrokeshire - and they look down to the mouth of the Teifi estuary.

Between the Preseli Hills' highest summit (Foel Cwm Cerwyn) and the second highest summit (Foel Eryr), the B4329 road from Haverfordwest to Cardigan crosses the curiously named Flemings Way, a prehistoric track that existed long before the Flemings arrived in Pembrokeshire. It was an important trade route for the copper and gold brought from the Wicklow Hills, and it runs for 6 miles along the Preseli ridge to descend at Crymych. The road from Crymych takes you through the north-eastern reaches of the Preseli Hills, to places such as Boncath, Cenarth Falls, Newcastle Emlyn and the beautiful Teifi Valley - one of the most scenic river valleys in Britain - which marks the boundaries between Pembrokeshire, Cardiganshire and Carmarthenshire. Apart from the famous salmon leap falls of Cenarth, the attractions in this captivating area include the Teifi Valley Railway, Cilgerran Castle and the Welsh Wildlife Centre.

Like any upland area, the Preseli Hills are best explored on foot, and apart from sheep the most common species you are likely to encounter in these wilds are hill walkers. Ornithologists, botanists, archaeologists, artists, photographers and others of strange pursuits also seem to find the hills a suitable habitat. However, unless you are familiar with the hills, it is advisable to take a map and compass on your travels. The average rainfall on the hills is nearly twice as much as it is on the coast, and the mists have a tendency to come down very suddenly. This is also the only part of Pembrokeshire where winter snow falls on anything like a regular basis.

An alternative way of exploring the Preseli Hills is to join a guided walk or horse riding session. These are run throughout the year by the National Park Authority as part of its annual activities and events programme. For more information contact any National Park Information Centre, or pick up a copy of the Authority's excellent free newspaper, Coast to Coast, which is produced especially for visitors and is widely available across the county.

The following is a brief survey of some of the villages and places of interest which lie on or near the slopes of the Preseli Hills and which have not been described in other parts of this guide.

Llys-y-fran Reservoir & Country Park

Close to the picturesque village of Rosebush, beautiful Llys-y-fran Country Park incorporates the 212-acre reservoir which supplies most of Pembrokeshire's drinking water. Around this man-made lake are mature woodlands and open grassland, with superb views of the Preseli Hills and surrounding farmland. In spring, the carpets of bluebells in the woods are a sheer delight, and throughout the season the country park is vibrant with the colours of countless varieties of wild flowers.

In recent years improvements have been made to the park, following a scheme to increase the size of the reservoir. For example, there is now a much wider footpath right round the reservoir, and 20,000 broad-leafed trees have been planted. As a result, the 7-mile perimeter walk is now even more enjoyable than ever. Regardless of how many visitors are in the park, you can always find a quiet spot to appreciate the fine views or enjoy a picnic at one of the many viewing areas. And if you prefer a shorter walk, you can take a stroll along the reservoir bank or the dam wall, where there is always something to see - a trout being landed, children learning to windsurf or sail, or the reservoir being re-stocked with fish.

Near the main car park is the children's adventure playground. This is equipped to keep youngsters amused for hours, giving you the ideal opportunity to pop into the nearby restaurant for a cup of tea or to browse around the gift shop.

Mountain bikes are another treat the kids will enjoy. Bikes can be hired by the hour or by the day, and with the reservoir perimeter path serving as a cycle track, this is a fun activity in which the whole family can participate.

Fishing is another leisure pursuit which has always been popular here, and Llys-y-fran attracts anglers from all over Wales and beyond. This is not surprising, as few fisheries can match the country park's excellent facilities. These include a purpose-built boathouse with a fleet of loch-style petrol-engine fishing boats - ideal for fly fishermen. During the season, over 30,000 top-quality rainbow trout are released into the freedom of the lake from their rearing cages. A healthy population of brown trout adds variety to the sport.

For watersports enthusiasts, the reservoir is perfect both for beginners and for more experienced sailors - particularly when the sea is too rough - but you must bring your own craft, as no hire is available. The park shop does however offer launching permits for dinghies, sailboards and canoes.

As you would expect in a country park of Llys-y-fran's status and reputation, wildlife is of prime concern in the management of the park. The oak and coniferous woodlands and rough grass provide ideal habitats for a variety of birds. More than 140 species have been recorded here, and during late autumn and winter the reservoir is the perfect haunt to spot wintering wildfowl. Mallard, teal and coot are among the regular visitors, while tufted duck, pochard, goldeneye, scaup, common scoter, goosander, long-tailed duck and little and great-crested grebe have all been seen here over the years. The reservoir's permanent predators, who are present all year round and compete with anglers for the reservoir's fish stocks, are the heron and cormorant.

Llys-y-fran's licensed restaurant enjoys superb views across the reservoir and countryside, and is housed in the Visitor Centre alongside the gift and souvenir shop. The restaurant offers excellent service and opens throughout the season, serving morning coffee, lunches, cream teas and evening meals. Sunday lunches are very popular, and the evening a la carte menu is well known for its choice and quality. If you wish to use the restaurant for Sunday lunch or an evening meal it is advisable to book in advance.

It is also worth noting that Llys-y-fran Country Park has strong historical and

musical connections. Near the base of the reservoir dam is a tumbledown cottage - the birthplace of the famous Welsh composer William 'Penfro' Rowlands. It was in gratitude for his son's recovery from a serious illness that he was inspired to write the tune for Blaenwern, one of the best loved of all hymn tunes. A monument to William Rowlands, erected by Welsh Water, now stands near the ruins of the old cottage.

For further information phone: 01437 532273/532694

Rosebush

Rosebush enjoys an unusual if modest claim to fame - slates from its quarries were used to roof the Houses of Parliament. But the village could have become a well-known tourist attraction in the 19th century, had everything gone according to plan. When the Clunderwen-Maenclochog railway opened in 1876 to serve the quarry there were big ambitions to develop Rosebush as an inland spa. A small tourist industry did develop here, but nothing like on the scale imagined.

Rosebush is close to Llysyfran Reservoir and Country Park and stands below the summit of Foel Cwm Cerwyn, in a superb setting which is ideal for walking. In 1992 a visitor centre and museum was opened in the village's old post office.

Mynachlogddu

This small pastoral community of the Preseli Hills once belonged to the monastery at St. Dogmael's. It stands east of Rosebush, close to the impressive Gors Fawr Stone Circle, which is over 70 feet in diameter. A commemorative stone to the poet Waldo Williams is also nearby.

New Moat

This small village stands in the Preseli foothills, just east of Llysyfran Country Park. A mound marks the site of a Norman motte and bailey castle. The church, distinctive for its tall tower, has an early 17th-century altar tomb.

Maenclochog

A small Victorian church on the village green is the central feature of this sprawling community on the southern slopes of the Preseli Hills, a couple of miles north-east of Llysyfran Country Park. For many years the village has served the needs of the area, and early this century Maenclochog boasted a blacksmith, miller, carpenter, lime burner, wheelwright,

draper, and no fewer than 10 pubs! A mile from the village is Penrhos - the only thatched cottage in the area, and now a museum.

Crymych

Crymych, situated on the A478 Tenby-Cardigan road, is a 19th-century hillside village which grew up around the railway. The Whitland-Cardigan line was completed in 1880 and no longer exists, but the village has remained an important agricultural centre and is an ideal base from which to explore the Preseli Hills. Within easy reach are Foel Drygarn, where cairns and an early Iron Age fort are to be found, and the 1300-feet summit of Y Frenni Fawr.

Boncath

Between Crymych and Newcastle Emlyn, Boncath takes it name from the

Pentre Ifan

Welsh word for buzzard. A former railway village, it is notable for two houses - Ffynone, designed by John Nash in 1792, and Cilwendeg, a Georgian house built by Morgan Jones.

Eglwyswrw

A compact little village near Castell Henllys Iron Age fort, north of the Preseli Hills, this place with the unpronounceable name (at least, to the English!) is where St. Wrw is buried. The pre-Christian churchyard is circular, and other interesting historical features include the medieval inn, the remains of a motte and bailey castle, and a prehistoric ringwork.

Castell Henllys Iron Age Fort : To visit Castell Henllys, just off the A487 a few miles east of Newport, is to travel back in time 2400 years. This remarkable and archaeologically important example of an Iron Age fort is managed by the National Park Authority and has been partially reconstructed with thatched roundhouses, animal pens, a smithy and a grain store, all standing on their original sites.

Castell Henllys

The new Visitor Centre houses an exhibition which serves as an introduction to the life of the early Celts in Wales. Castell Henllys probably flourished between the 4th century BC and 1st century AD, when the Romans began their conquest of Britain. The Iron Age Celts were a fierce and warlike people, and many of their chieftains lived in well-defended forts, of which Castell Henllys was typical. Sited on a valley spur, it had natural defences on three sides, and where the spur joined the side of the valley massive earthworks were thrown up, topped with timber palisades. Stone walling protected a narrow gateway which can still be seen. Such elaborate defences would have employed a huge labour force, and this suggests that Castell Henllys was occupied by a leader of some importance, along with family, retainers and even a band of warriors.

The introduction to the site of domestic animals which flourished in the Iron Age has given a further insight into the daily life of these ancient ancestors. A self-guided trail takes you through Castell Henllys, with informative interpretative panels along the way. This is a wonderful place for schools and study groups, and a new Education Centre has been built in the valley below the fort. To further recapture the atmosphere and spirit of this mystical historic site, which stands in beautiful North Pembrokeshire countryside below the summit of Carn Ingli, special events are held throughout the holiday season, including shows given by the Prytani - an Iron Age Celtic re-enactment group. Castell Henllys is open daily from Easter to October. For further information ring 01239 891319.

The Landsker Borderlands

When the Normans invaded Pembroke in 1093 and took the site on which the magnificent castle now stands, they were quick to consolidate their domination of South Pembrokeshire and the lands they had gained here. To the north of the county the rebellious Welsh proved more troublesome. The Norman response was to build a line of castles to protect their new-won territory, effectively dividing north from south.

These formidable fortresses stretched from Llanstephan in the southeast to Roch in the northwest. They marked what has become known as the Landsker Line - a word of Norse origin meaning frontier. Originally a military device, the Landsker evolved into a cultural and linguistic divide, and its effects are evident even today. For example, in the north of the county Welsh is still spoken and many of the place names are Welsh also. Churches are usually small, with bellcotes and no towers. By comparison, in the anglicised south English is the dominant language, as is clear from the names of the towns and villages, and the Norman churches are characterised by tall, square towers which served as lookouts.

One of the castles of the Landsker Line was Narberth. Its scant ruins still stand near the centre of this important market town, which is 10 miles north of Tenby. Narberth is at the heart of a beautiful and historic part of inland Pembrokeshire known as the Landsker Borderlands. The Borderlands spill over into old Carmarthenshire and are bounded by the River Taf to the east, the Daugleddau estuary to the west, hills and valleys to the

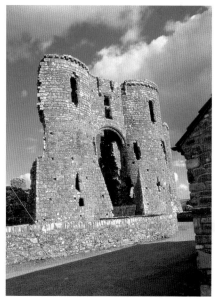

Llawhaden Castle

north and vales and plains to the south. As awareness of the Borderlands increases, a growing number of visitors are exploring this largely undiscovered area of great rural delights.

The attractive countryside of the Landsker Borderlands, rich in heritage and wildlife, is typified in the north by lush farmland sweeping down from the Preseli Hills. Here you will discover quiet river valleys and tranquil riverside communities, such as those of Lawrenny and Landshipping on the upper reaches of the Daugleddau estuary.

South of the Landsker, the rural landscape belies its industrial past. It is hard to believe, for example, that small villages like Reynalton and Jeffreston were once at the heart of the thriving Pembrokeshire coalfield.

Like all Pembrokeshire, the Landsker Borderlands display evidence of a long history and of occupation by very early settlers. There are prehistoric sites at

Holgan Camp, Llawhaden - an Iron Age hillfort - and remains of settlements in Canaston Woods, near Canaston Bridge. Medieval ruins are plentiful, including the Sisters House in ancient Minwear Woods, the hospice chapel and castle-cum-bishop's palace in Llawhaden, and the mighty Norman castles of Carew and Manorbier.

The Borderlands are also a natural draw for all who appreciate wildlife. During spring and summer the hedgerows and woodlands are ablaze with the colours of snowdrops, primroses, campions, cowslips, foxgloves, bluebells, dog roses, cow parsley, honeysuckle and many varieties of common and rare orchids. In autumn, fungi and ferns brighten the woodland floor, and butterflies, moths and damselflies bring dashes of colour to the air. Birds and mammals are in abundance too. Buzzards, tawny owls, grey herons, kingfishers, woodpeckers and numerous

Llawhaden Church

species of waders and dippers can all be seen in the Borderlands, along with foxes, badgers and even elusive otters. In spring, you might also spot the rare Tenby daffodil, which is particular to this area.

There are many ways to enjoy the picturesque countryside and diverse wildlife of the Landsker Borderlands. You can walk, cycle or ride on horseback, or pursue interests such as fishing, painting, photography or bird watching, or discover the secrets of traditional rural crafts such as pottery and lovespoon making. Whatever your chosen route, you will find an intriguing and beautiful part of Pembrokeshire that is still unknown to many.

Walking

Walking is the ideal way to see the Landsker Borderlands, taking full advantage of the area's excellent network of footpaths, bridleways and quiet country

Walking in the Landsker

lanes. Many of the more attractive footpaths have been identified with the help of local villagers, and these routes often pass sites of historical interest and outstanding natural beauty. For more serious walkers, the 52-mile Landsker Borderlands Trail links all the major villages of the Borderlands, offering a great variety of landscape and local heritage and culture. The walk is described, with full directions, in a series of full-colour walking cards now available from Tourist Information Centres, The Landsker Visitor Centre and other outlets.

Even longer is the South Pembrokeshire Trail. This 70-mile circular route combines three long-distance walks in one - southern sections of the Pembrokeshire Coastal Path, the Landsker Borderlands Trail and a trail known as The Knightsway.

Another option - and a very popular one with walkers - is to book a tailor-made package holiday through Landsker Countryside Holidays. Accommodation along the route is booked ahead and as you progress your luggage is transferred for you.

Cycling

The area of the Landsker Borderlands is relatively flat, so cycling is as practical as it is enjoyable. It is also an ideal way to get off the beaten track and discover the nooks and crannies and small rural communities which make this region of Pembrokeshire such a pleasure to explore. Furthermore, with so many country pubs and tearooms at your disposal, you can easily plan your own route, whether you are looking for a day's outing or a holiday dedicated to cycling. You can also join an organised holiday, with all arrangements taken care of, including accommodation booked ahead, luggage transfer and even a rescue service!

Horse Riding

The Landsker countryside is well endowed with leafy bridle ways, giving access to woodlands and forestry as well as open country. Riding holidays and daily lessons and rides are well catered for in the area, made even more popular by the many wide sandy beaches of South Pembrokeshire, which are perfect riding territory. Many such holidays include accommodation.

Fishing

Coarse, game or sea fishing: whatever type of angling you favour, the Landsker countryside can show you excellent facilities. There are numerous well-stocked lakes in quiet rural locations, and the Taf and Cleddau rivers provide a first-class challenge for trout, sewin and salmon. For sea anglers, South Pembrokeshire's coastline is a popular and lucrative hunting ground, whether you fish from the beach, harbour or boat. And, as with cycling and walking, you can turn your favourite leisure pursuit into an organised holiday, with package deals which include accommodation.

Rural Crafts

Traditional crafts are still much in evidence in South Pembrokeshire. Pottery, slate working, glass blowing, weaving, basketry, wood-turning and carving are all demonstrated to visitors in the studios and workshops of local craftspeople and artists. There are many opportunities for you to try your own hand at some of these crafts - particularly if you book a Landsker Countryside Holiday, which can include a crafts weekend.

Greenways

Each summer a series of guided walks from the railway stations enable visitors to make use of local transport to experience the beauty of the countryside under the leadership of a qualified local guide.

Heritage

South Pembrokeshire villages and hamlets are blessed with a wealth of heritage and have their stories to tell. Visitors can explore rich and varied themes by selecting one or more of the `Makers of Wales' trail guides.

The seven themes of the 'Makers of Wales' campaign offer an opportunity to explore the South Pembrokeshire and Daugleddau areas by car, cycle or foot. Themes include 'Chieftains & Princes', 'Arts & Literature', 'Shaping the Landscape', 'Myth, Legend & Faith', 'Transport & Communications', 'A future from our past' and 'Makers of Wales - Industry, Energy & Enterprise'.

Gelli

Landsker Countryside Holidays: are working with a wide range of accommodation to link the trails into short or long breaks.For further information on the Landsker Borderlands, ring SPARC on 01834 860965.

The Pembroke Coast Line

North Beach, Tenby

There is so much to see and do in Pembrokeshire regardless of the weather or the kind of activity you're into. But have you ever thought of leaving the car at home and discovering the towns and villages, beaches, historic sites and the many country and coastal walks that you can reach using the train.

Train services on the Pembroke Coast Line are operated by Wales and West. It is the ideal way to discover a diversity of local attractions and interesting landmarks beginning its journey by leaving the main line at the country market town of Whitland.

Whitland is an excellent place to set off to see the Landsker Borderlands if you wish, rich in historical sites and an ideal retreat, offering open countryside, serene woodlands and the peace and tranquility of the upper reaches of the Daugleddau Estuary and the secluded Taf Valley. From Whitland, the line meanders west along the tranquil Lampeter Vale offering stunning views across open pasture and the woods on the hill around Llanddewi Velfrey

before arriving at Narberth, a small, busy market town complemented by an excellent range of individual shops, art and craft galleries, pubs and cafes. There are some good walks in the surrounding countryside and Narberth makes a good touring centre.

After Narberth tunnel, the train heads south towards the coast. Kilgetty, the next stop is a former mining village and just 2 miles from the coast. With it's tourist information centre and good amenities, Kilgetty is worth visiting and it has the added benefit of being close to several major attractions such as Folly Farm, Begelly Pottery and Grove Colliery. All these places can be reached form Kilgetty by bus. A short journey further south along the line brings you to Saundersfoot, with the station itself being about 1 miles from the main village. There is a frequent bus service from Tenby to the centre of Saundersfoot, though if you're feeling like some fresh air you may wish to walk down the 'Incline', a former colliery railway track which takes you into the village. Saundersfoot itself has excellent beaches and a large harbour, sheltered from the open sea by two large stone breakwaters. It is within the harbour car park that you will find the information centre - a former coal tally office.

If you continue on the train from here you're next main stop is the historic town of Tenby - a haven for first class beaches and facilities alike. Tenby is the major holiday resort for the area, flanked by four magnificent beaches and leads via a network of narrow and picturesque streets and alleyways to its small harbour, where boat trips depart to the monastic island of Caldey and all along the coast. Dramatic coastal views can be enjoyed in all directions and there are a multitude of interesting places to visit including the National Trust's Merchant Tudor House, Tenby Museum and Art Gallery and St.

Mill Pond, Pembroke

Mary's Church. The Leisure Centre is situated in Marsh Road, about 1 mile from the station, and includes a swimming pool.

To continue on the line, takes you behind the dunes of South Beach and into the tranquil village of Penally. The station is very convenient for the village and for the level walk to the quiet end of South Beach (about 300 yards). The village of Penally itself has three pubs and a useful shop/post office (see page 32). Remaining tantalisingly close to the coast, the line takes you ever further west through the next rural stations of Manorbier and Lamphey. The station at Manorbier is about a mile from the village, though buses can be taken to the village from Penally and Lamphey for those who would prefer not to walk. Manorbier has a superb beach for surfing and swimming whilst the station at Lamphey, a few miles further down the line gives direct access to village facilities and the nearby church. (see page 40).

The final two stops on this fascinating line are Pembroke and Pembroke Dock. The ancient town of Pembroke is an excellent touring centre for South Pembrokeshire with a wide range of accommodation, interesting shops and restaurants. For more information on Pembroke see page 42, however, possibly the best way to see the town is to follow the town trail booklet available from the information centre on the commons.

The line ends at Pembroke Dock, site of the former Royal Dockyard. It has a wide range of shops and the Martello tower just off Front Street has been developed as an interpretation centre where the past and the present are brought to life. Pembroke Dock is the major ferry port for Rosslare in Ireland and there are often excellent special day excursion offers, so it is worth checking them out. Irish Ferries can be contacted on 0990 329543.

The Pembroke Coast line is an excellent way to view South Pembrokeshire and to reach points along the coast path. Tickets can be purchased from the conductor on the train, however if you want to stop off at a number of places, the Greenways Day Ranger ticket is good value. This provides unlimited rail travel on the Whitland to Pembroke Dock line for a whole day (not available on any Saturday from June to September) and costs £3.50 for adults and £1.75 for children. These can be bought on the train.

You can use the train to reach many lovely walks in Pembrokeshire. A number of leaflets detailing specific walks such as the Landsker Borderlands and Guided Walks from Railway Stations are available for Tourist Information Centres or by contacting SPARC (South Pembrokeshire Partnership for Action with Rural Communities) on 01834 860965. For information regarding train times and fares contact 0870 9000 773. For a complimentary Pocket Timetable (code K) by post, please call 0870 9000 772. Coastal Path information is available from the Pembrokeshire Coast National Authority on 01437 764636.

Narberth

Distances: Fishguard 24, Haverfordwest 9, Milford Haven 14, Pembroke 15, St. David's 25, Tenby 10, Carmarthen 21 & London 241.

Administrative centre of the borderlands, the market town of Narberth stands just south of the Landsker, in what is regarded as 'Little England beyond Wales', but has its roots buried deep in Welsh history, culture and tradition.

The Welsh princes of Dyfed lived here in the Dark Ages and the town - then called Arberth - features in the ancient stories of The Mabinogion.

Narberth is also remembered for the infamous Rebecca Riots of the 19th century. These began in 1839 with the burning of toll gates in Efailwen, a hamlet in the Preseli foothills a few miles north of the town. This anger was in response to the decision by rich landowners to impose crippling road tolls on the small and impoverished farming communities. The men responsible for torching the toll gates avoided recognition by dressing in women's clothing and blackening their faces, and they addressed their leader as 'Rebecca'. The dispute quickly became more widespread and other toll gates were destroyed just as quickly as they could be erected. The riots, often described as a 'true people's revolt' because they had their cause in natural justice, went on for a period of several years. It is one of the ironies of local history that when the authorities called out the troops in a bid to discover the identity of Rebecca and his followers, they were billeted in Narberth's poorhouse.

Narberth Castle, of which little now remains, was part of the Norman frontier separating north from south. It was captured by the Welsh on numerous occasions and destroyed in the Civil War by Cromwell's forces. The castle ruins are currently under restoration and are open to visitors in the summer months.

Narberth's small but attractive town centre is distinctive for its Town Hall - the former Landsker Visitor Centre - and pleasant Georgian houses. With the promotion of the Landsker Borderlands and other rural tourist areas, Narberth has been revitalised. SPARC - South Pembrokeshire Action for Rural Communities - has its headquarters here, and the town is very close to a number of the county's most popular attractions. The list is impressive: Heron's Brook Leisure Park, Oakwood, Canaston Centre, Blackpool Mill, Picton Castle, Llawhaden Castle, Holgan Camp Iron Age hillfort and Folly Farm. These are in addition to those places of interest in Narberth itself, which

Narberth

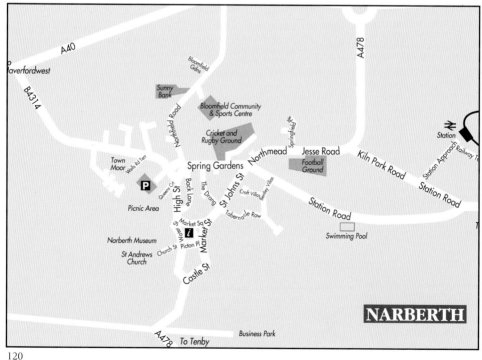

include the Landsker Visitor Centre, Wilson Museum and Golden Sheaf Gallery.

Heron's Brook Leisure Park & Approach Golf Course: A countryside attraction near the centre of Narberth, the park is set in 30 acres of parkland and offers a good family day out. For keen and budding golfers, there's the challenge of 9-hole pitch & putt and an 18-hole approach golf course. For more information ring 01834 860723.

Canaston Bridge

Just west of Narberth, Canaston Bridge marks the junction of the A40 and A4075. This attractive wooded area is the northern boundary of the Eastern Cleddau, and from here you can join the Knightsway - a 9-mile walk linking the Daugleddau Trail with the coast path at Amroth. Nearby, on the south side of the A40, is a picnic area and restored Blackpool Mill, and a mile or so from the north side is the impressive ruin of Llawhaden Castle. A few miles south, on the A4075, are the neighbouring attractions of Oakwood and Canaston Centre. Also within the area are several interesting woodland walks, including a relatively short path which takes you to Blackpool Mill.

Oakwood & CC2000: See page 143

Blackpool Mill

In a beautiful setting on the banks of the Eastern Cleddau, this is one of the finest examples in Wales of a mill complete with all of its machinery. This has been restored and can be seen in motion. Other attractions here include coracles and a wheelwright's shop. For more information ring 01437 541233.

Clunderwen

Situated just inside Carmarthenshire and known until the 1870's as Narberth

Blackpool Mill

Road. The village of Clunderwen developed with the coming of the railway in 1852. An interesting historical anecdote is that it was here in 1913 that the James Brothers first flew their bi-plane - one of the earliest flights in Wales.

Efailwen

A small community north of Narberth, in the southern Preseli foothills, Efailwen is recorded in the history books as the place where the erection of a toll gate in 1839 sparked off the Rebecca Riots. Nearby, at Glandy Cross, is a group of Neolithic and Bronze Age sites, regarded as the most important in South Wales.

Gelli

Located just north of Llawhaden, the small community of Gelli developed around a large woollen mill. This worked from the late 19th century until 1937, and was one of several mills which flourished in the Landsker Borderlands at that time. Fishing was another important industry here. In the late 19th century 6 pairs of

Cleddau coracles fished between Gelli and Llawhaden.

Lampeter Velfrey

It is thought that the Landsker Line, were it ever drawn, would pass through the parish of Lampeter Velfrey, which is a few miles due east of Narberth. There are several prehistoric sites in the immediate area, including tumuli, a Bronze Age hearth and 3 Neolithic burial chambers.

Llanboidy

Llanboidy lies across the border in old Carmarthenshire, about 5 miles north of Whitland, in the small Gronw Valley. A well in the village was the focus of many medieval pilgrimages, and close to Llanboidy are two ancient sites - a cromlech at Cefn Brafle and Arthur's Table, a tumulus, which is in a wood at Dolwilym. Today the village enjoys fame as the home of Pemberton's Victorian Chocolates.

Llanddewi Velfrey

Located between Narberth and Whitland on the busy A40, Llanddewi Velfrey originally grew around its ancient church, and there is evidence of occupation during the Iron Age. The Quaker burial ground also reflects a strong tradition of non-conformity. The area around the village is ideal for country walks, with stunning views of the Marlais Valley to the south and the Preseli Hills to the north.

Llandissilio

This village stands on the A478 north of Narberth, a road which has developed from a prehistoric route that linked the Preseli Hills and the Cleddau estuary. Castle sites and earthworks suggest that the parish has a long history - an idea supported by the inscribed stones in the

church which date from the 5th or 6th century.

Llawhaden

Llawhaden was an important medieval settlement standing on the Landsker Line, and the original Norman castle was later developed as a magnificent bishop's palace by the Bishops of St. David's. The ruins which stand today are evidence of the grandeur of this fortified palatial residence. You can also see the remains of a medieval hospice chapel. The Norman church of St. Aidan stands in the valley below, on the banks of the Eastern Cleddau, in a very picturesque position.

Llawhaden Castle

Originally a wooden structure built in Norman times, the castle was rebuilt by the Bishops of St. David's between the late 13th and 15th centuries and transformed into a great-fortified palace. This comprised several buildings set around a five-sided courtyard, strengthened with angled corners. The ruins, now in the care of Cadw (Welsh Historic Monuments), include the front of the gatehouse, which still stands to its full height, the Great Hall, bakehouse, barracks, visitors' lodgings and the Chapel of the Blessed Virgin. After using the castle for more than 250 years, the bishops dismantled it and stripped the lead from the roof. Close to the castle are two other historic attractions - a restored medieval hospice and Holgan Camp, an Iron Age fort to which visitors now have access thanks to the opening of a new public footpath. The site of the camp was overgrown for centuries until cleared and fenced by SPARC - the South Pembrokeshire Partnership for Action with Rural Communities - and Cadw. Holgan Camp had formidable defences, and is a well-preserved example of an Iron Age

Lawrenny

defended enclosure. Many such camps were established in this area.

Ludchurch

Located less than 3 miles south-east of Narberth, Ludchurch stands on the route of the Knightsway footpath. A curious fact is that prior to the 1950's, the name Ludchurch referred only to the Norman church and parish, and the village itself was known as Egypt! There are definitely no pyramids here, but there are some fine limekilns to be seen in the old quarry, which today is a beautifully landscaped area. The name Ludchurch is also becoming increasingly well known among people with good taste. The reason is Princes Gate Water - spring water of exceptionally pure quality which in just 4 years has proven so popular that it is now supplied all over Wales and to markets as far apart as London and North America.

The water comes from 3 acres of farmland in the parish which are saturated with clear natural springs.

Reynalton

Reynalton, situated west of Begelly and south of Narberth, is now a small, quiet hamlet in the midst of farmland. Yet earlier in the century coal mining was a thriving local industry, as the village stands in the old South Pembrokeshire coalfield.

Robeston Wathen

The earliest record of Robeston Wathen dates back to 1282. The small hill-top community, on the A40, has a Norman church and its distinctive tower.

Tavernspite

Tavernspite is on the Pembrokeshire-Carmarthenshire border at the junction of the B4328 and B4314. At one time this was also on the route of the mail coaches which travelled from London to Ireland via Milford Haven. The local community here takes great pride in the village; in recent years Tavernspite has won awards in competitions for Wales In Bloom and Best Kept Village. Tavernspite is also notable for its chapel - one of the most remote and picturesque in Pembrokeshire.

Templeton

The layout of Templeton, which is a mile south of Narberth, is a fine example of village planning in the Middle Ages. It is believed that the Knights Templars had a hospice here - possibly on the site now occupied by St. John's church - and in the 13th century the village was known as the settlement of the Templars. Hence the name Templeton today. There are several ancient sites here, including Sentence Castle, originally a raised fortification which also probably dates from the time of the Knights Templars. The Knightsway trail passes through the village.

Barn Court Antiques, Templeton: Situated on the A478 Tenby road at Templeton, close to the Boar's Head public house. Barn Court Antiques, now in its 12th year specialises in fine quality 18th and 19th Century furniture together with a varied selection of china and decorative items. The Tea room offers morning coffee, light meals and afternoon teas with the emphasis on home-made cakes, which can be served either on the flower decked verandah or in the relaxing Tea-Room. A selection of crafts and collectables complement the Tea-Room. Open all year, 10:00am - 5:00pm including Saturday and Sunday. (Closed Mondays during winter months). Proprietors: David, Anne and Martyn Evans.

The Daugleddau

The Daugleddau estuary is an area of great natural beauty, comprising the fascinating stretch of waterway which extends inland from the Haven and encompasses four rivers - Western Cleddau, Eastern Cleddau, Carew and Cresswell. It is an inner sanctuary, often described as the hidden treasure of the Pembrokeshire Coast National Park.Daugleddau (which means two rivers of the Cleddau) begins east of the Cleddau toll bridge, beyond the reach of the supertankers and shipping lanes of Milford Haven. It flows through the rural landscape to places of great tranquillity, and is so often overlooked by visitors that it has become known as The Secret Waterway.

The waterway is characterised by steep wooded sides and small sheltered inlets, known as pills. The estuarine shoreline, with its salt marsh vegetation and tidal and mud flats, provides a rich habitat for plants and animals and is an important winter feeding ground for waders and waterfowl. Goldeneye, red-breasted merganser and curlew are all attracted here, as are shelduck, cormorants, herons, kingfishers and many other species.waterway also boasts some of the best deciduous woodland within the National Park. Oak, ash and sycamore support a variety of woodland birds and mammals - from woodpeckers and tawny owls to bats, badgers and secretive otters.

In spring and summer, roadside hedgerows become a bouquet of wild flowers - primroses, early purple orchids, bluebells, red campion, honeysuckle and foxgloves.

In recognition of the Daugleddau's remarkable diversity of flora and fauna, many parts of the waterway are designated Sites of Special Scientific Interest. These include the Carew and Cresswell rivers,

Carew Castle

Lawrenny Wood, Minwear Wood, parts of Slebech Park, and West Williamston Quarries.

The serenity of the Daugleddau belies a history coloured by centuries of maritime trade and stained by the toil of coalminers and quarrymen.

In Tudor times Lawrenny was famous for its oysters. By the 19th century sailing vessels of all shapes and sizes - brigantines, ketches, sloops, schooners and coasters - were busily importing and exporting coal, culm, grain, limestone, timber and general goods. Towards the latter part of the century, Willy Boys - flat, barge-like craft - carried local produce and ran a shuttle service between seagoing vessels and the Daugleddau's upper reaches.

The poor acidic soils of West Wales made lime a valuable and highly saleable commodity. Limestone was quarried at West Williamston, Garron Pill and Llangwm Ferry and burned in hundreds of kilns along the waterway and coastline, from South Pembrokeshire to Cardigan Bay. The remains of several kilns are still visible.

The band of carboniferous coal measures which runs across Pembrokeshire from St. Bride's Bay to Saundersfoot cuts through the uppermost reaches of the Daugleddau, and mining around Landshipping was at its height in the first half of 19th century - particularly after the introduction in 1800 of the first steam engine to be used in a Pembrokeshire coalfield. The high-quality anthracite was in great demand. But a tragic accident at the Garden Pit near Landshipping in 1844, and a series of insurmountable geological problems which plagued the coalfield throughout its working life, led to a rapid decline of the industry by the early 20th century. The last colliery to work, at Hook

on the Western Cleddau, was closed by the National Coal Board in 1949.

The waterway's rich oak woodlands helped encourage boatbuilding, and cutters, smacks and schooners were built at yards and quays along the Daugleddau. At Lawrenny alone, over 40 sailing vessels were built during the first half of the 19th century.

Other industries flourished too - from a chemical works at Whalecomb to a furnace and forge which operated on the site now occupied by Blackpool Mill. And during the 19th century over 100 men earned their living by compass net fishing - a traditional method, suited to rivers with fast-flowing tidal currents, which required considerable skill and courage.

Much of the working life of the Daugleddau centred around Lawrenny Quay, which in its heyday had more than one quay. Today it is noted for its Yacht

Station and excellent facilities for pleasure craft, and seeing the waterway from the comfort of a boat will take you to places inaccessible by any other means.

But whatever your method of exploration, the Daugleddau will provide endless relaxation and enjoyment.

Sights worth seeking out are many and varied, and include Lawrenny village and its well-restored cottages and huge Norman church. A National Park picnic site gives superb views over the Carew and Cresswell rivers.

At Cresswell Quay, a picnic site and pub are just yards from the water's edge, where kingfishers and herons feed in full view.

The long-distance Daugleddau Trail and other footpaths reveal a succession of delights, from the evocative ruins of magnificent Carew Castle to the ancient woodland of Minwear.

And there are many other historic sites to enjoy, such as the exotic gardens of Upton Castle and Picton Castle and the restored mills at Carew and Blackpool.

The limestone quarries have long since fallen silent, but today West Williamston is the centre of other important work for the waterway - the rescue, nursing and rehabilitation of injured and contaminated seabirds, at the Oiled Bird Rescue Centre. Regular visitors to the centre each year are substantial numbers of Manx shearwaters, which once blown inland by autumn gales are unable to take off again and are often stranded in brightly-lit harbours and resorts such as Tenby.

Burton

Sitting just across the Cleddau toll bridge from Pembroke Dock, and close to Neyland, Burton is a small hillside village which enjoys superb views over the waterway. It is best known as a boating centre and for its popular waterfront pub,

which as well as good food boasts a large beer garden and panoramic views over the estuary to the south, east and west.

Canaston Bridge

See page 143

Carew

The most southerly point of the Daugleddau section of the National Park, Carew is famous for its magnificent riverside castle, fine Celtic cross and restored tidal mill. There is also a picnic site and car park here, accessible from the village across the old narrow bridge. The village itself is small, neat and has a distinct charm, with a pub and a restaurant offering plenty of local hospitality. Close to Carew, on the south side of the A477, is the slumbering hamlet of Carew Cheriton. The church here dates from the late 14th century and is distinctive for its very tall tower, which has a corner steeple. In the churchyard there is a detached mortuary chapel.

Carew Castle

Here is a castle which has everything: magnificent ruins, an evocative setting, a long and important history, examples of medieval and Elizabethan architecture, a Celtic cross which is one of the finest in Wales, archaeological deposits dating back over the last 2000 years - and (what castle is complete without them?) two ghosts!

Carew is undoubtedly a king among castles. It stands on a low limestone ridge at the head of a tidal inlet of the Carew River - a strategic position, as it guarded a crossing of the river and the main road to Pembroke, 5 miles away. In times of war it could also be supplied by boat, as it had access to the open sea via the Daugleddau and the Haven waterway.

Carew Castle was occupied continuously from the 12th century to the end of the 17th century, during which time it was gradually transformed from a medieval fortress to an Elizabethan mansion of considerable splendour. Most photographs today tend to emphasis the latter, as the castle is often shot from across the water of Carew Pill to capture one of the ruin's most striking features - the great Renaissance north wing which Sir John Perrot began building in 1588. Perrot died in 1592 of natural causes while imprisoned in the Tower of London, and the wing was never completed.

In April 1507 the castle and nearby Carew Meadows were the site of the Great Tournament - a spectacular 5-day event, attended by over 600 noblemen. The occasion was in honour of the Tudor monarchy and also to celebrate the fact that Henry VII had bestowed upon Sir Rhys ap Thomas, who held the castle at that time, the Order of the Knight of the

Garter. (Sir Rhys had played a major part in Henry's victory at Bosworth and was knighted on the battlefield; it is even said that Richard III died at his hands). Although the king himself was not in attendance, the tournament was a grand affair, on a scale not previously seen in Wales. The huge assembly enjoyed jousting, sword displays, hunting and other sports of the day, and the Great Hall was the scene of a sumptuous banquet. This was the last event of its kind ever staged in Britain.

During the Civil War years of 1644 and 1645, the castle changed hands between royalist and parliamentarian forces no fewer than four times. Towards the end of the century, it was abandoned by the Carew family and fell into decline.

The history of any castle which enjoyed such a long period of occupancy is obviously complex, involving many families, characters and events. But the exciting thing about Carew Castle is that much is still being discovered about its very early history. Since 1986 it has been the subject of a phased but intensive archaeological survey involving excavation, a stone-by-stone study of the surviving walls and buildings, and examination of documents. To date, two major surprises have been unearthed. One is that the Norman part of the castle is much bigger and older than previously suspected. The other is the discovery of pre-Norman fortifications, adding weight to speculation that the site had a royal significance long before the Normans arrived and was the seat of Welsh kings throughout the Roman and Dark Age periods. This idea is supported by the famous Carew Cross, which stands within the Castle Field and is a memorial to a Welsh king who died in 1035 - more than half a century before the Normans took Pembroke in 1093.

In the near future visitors to the castle will be able to see some of the discoveries made by the archaeological survey, as there are plans to build an Interpretation Centre on site. The castle is still privately owned by descendants of the Carew family, but is leased to the Pembrokeshire Coast National Park Authority under a 99-year agreement so that the castle and its surrounding earthworks can be conserved for everyone's enjoyment. Carew is the only castle managed by the National Park Authority. For more information ring 01646 651782.

Carew Cross

Carew's famous 11th-century Celtic Cross stands close to the castle. It is a royal memorial commemorating Maredudd ap Edwin, who in 1033 became joint ruler with his brother of Deheubarth, the kingdom of southwest Wales. Just two years later he was killed in battle. The

cross comprises two separate pieces and the inscriptions are predominantly Celtic but also reflect Scandinavian influence. For more information ring 01646 651782.

Carew Tidal Mill

This is the only tidal mill to remain intact in Wales, and it stands on the causeway which dams the 23-acre millpond. The present mill is 19th century but the site was previously occupied by a medieval building which operated in Elizabethan times. The mill's machinery was powered by water stored at flood tide and released through sluices to drive two undershot mill wheels. It continued to grind corn commercially until 1937 and was restored in 1972. Today it is often known as the French mill - a reference to either the architectural style of the building or the mill's grinding stones, which were imported from France. As with Carew Castle, the mill is managed by the National Park Authority. It is open to visitors throughout the summer and is a popular and fascinating attraction. For more information ring 01646 651657.

Upton Castle Grounds

Upton Castle grounds and gardens occupy a secluded wooded valley which runs down to a tributary of the Carew River. Since 1976 they have been managed and maintained by the Pembrokeshire Coast National Park Authority, and there is free parking on site. The grounds contain over 250 different species of trees and shrubs. For more information contact any National Park Information Centre.

Cresswell Quay

This is a beautiful spot for a picnic, or to enjoy a pint or Sunday lunch at the old riverside pub. The tidal Cresswell River attracts herons and a variety of other waders, and brilliantly coloured kingfishers

Celtic Cross, Carew

often catch the eye as they dive for prey and seek out the best perches along the banks. Across the water, high above the steep wooded slopes, buzzards soar effortlessly over the trees of Scotland Wood.

Hook

There is much evidence here of the area's long and intensive coalmining activities, including the remains of two quays, tramways, and bell-shaped mines from the 17th and 18th centuries. Hook Pit did not close until 1949, and in its later days was linked to the Milford Haven railway.is a small settlement on the eastern banks of the Daugleddau, near the confluence of the Western and Eastern Cleddau rivers. Across the river, close to Picton Point, is the site from which the Picton Ferry once operated. Coal was a valuable commodity here as the mining industry thrived for a period in the 19th century, and Landshipping Quay exported coal from several pits. Close by is the site of the terrible Garden Pit colliery disaster of 1844, when high tide flooded the mine and 40 lives were lost, including those of several young boys.

Lawrenny

Lawrenny has an impressive church with a large Norman tower. Using the site once occupied by Lawrenny Castle - an 18th-century mansion now demolished - the National Park Authority has established a picnic area, with superb views over the Daugleddau. Earlier this century, at Lawrenny Home Farm, Mr. J.F. Lort-Phillips trained racehorses and put the village on the map when Kirkland won the Grand National in 1905. Another horseracing connection is that nearby Coedcanlas was the birthplace of famous jockey turned bestselling author Dick Francis.

Lawrenny Quay

Close to Lawrenny village, Lawrenny Quay is an important yachting, boating and water-sports centre which once boasted a thriving shipbuilding industry. During the Second World War, Lawrenny Quay served as a marine air base for 764 Squadron of the Fleet Air Arm. Up to 15 Walrus seaplanes could be seen moored on the river, and the officers were billeted at Lawrenny Castle.

Llangwm

Llangwm has a long history, and is said to have been a Flemish settlement in the Middle Ages. Traditionally, the main occupations of the villagers were oyster and herring fishing, with mining rising in importance in the 19th century. Llangwm is well known for its reputedly tough breed of fisherwomen, who until this century were a familiar sight on Pembrokeshire

roads, carrying baskets of fish on their heads to sell in the towns. Near to Llangwm is Black Tar, a popular spot for boating and watersports enthusiasts.

Martletwy

A small agricultural community east of Landshipping, Martletwy is now the unlikely home of a vineyard - Cwm Deri - the only commercial vineyard in Pembrokeshire. Another product associated with Martletwy is coal, though this industry has long since vanished. Among the interesting historic buildings here is the church.

Minwear

A large area of the precious and ancient Minwear Wood is a designated SSSI - Site of Special Scientific Interest - and in the heart of the wood is the 12th-century church. Close by are the ruins of the medieval Sisters Houses, which once accommodated pilgrims bound for the monastic community at St. David's. Minwear Wood is close to Blackpool Mill and Canaston Bridge.

West Williamston

When the limestone quarries were established here, this medieval farming hamlet was transformed into a busy quarrymen's village with smithies, inns and its own church. Today the area has reverted to farming, and is also the home of the important Oiled Bird Rescue Centre.

The Oiled Bird Rescue Centre

A vital local resource because of the proximity of refineries and supertankers in the Milford Haven waterway. The Centre is funded entirely by voluntary contributions and welcomes visitors. For more information ring 01646 651236.

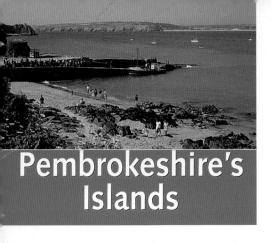

Pembrokeshire's Islands

Cardigan Island

A small island of less than 16 hectares, situated at the mouth of the River Teifi. The island is leased by Wales Wildlife Trust, who annually census its small colonies of seabirds. The lesser black-backed gulls are the dominant species, with only a few hundred herring gulls and very small numbers of other seabirds. In 1934, when the motor vessel Herefordshire was wrecked on the northern rocks, brown rats came ashore and annihilated the island's population of puffins. There have been various attempts to reinstate both puffins and Manx shearwaters; a few have bred but it is a long and slow process to establish healthy breeding colonies here again.

Ramsey Island

260 hectares of fascinating island, now accessible by a regular boat service from the lifeboat slip at St. Justinian's (about 3 miles west of St. David's), across the infamous but spectacular Ramsey Sound, with its equally infamous and treacherous reef known as The Bitches.

Ramsey was farmed until very recently. To the east, steep sheltered spring-fed valleys and cliffs are covered in a wonderful tangle of rich vegetation, and to the north-east are sheep-grazed fields which support perhaps the largest population of breeding lapwings in Wales.

Chough also find Ramsey extremely attractive, and both species breed and winter here in good numbers. The western coastline is rugged and spectacular, with two small 'mountains' (Carn Llundain and Carn Ysgubor) sheltering the island from the main blast of the prevailing westerly winds.

In the south, below Carn Llundain, lies a major seabird cliff. It is at least 450 feet high and is used by several thousand seabirds in the season, including razorbills, kittiwakes, fulmars and guillemots.

On a clear day the mountaintop views are superb. To the north and east are St. David's and the Preseli Hills; to the west, the rocks and islets of the Bishops and Clerks, and the main South Bishop rock, where Manx shearwaters and storm petrels breed; and to the south, the small offshore islands of Ynys Cantwr and Ynys Beri, with Skomer and Midland Isle beyond them across St. Bride's Bay.

The caves and beaches around Ramsey are breeding grounds for the largest population of grey seals in south-western Britain; more than 300 seal pups are born here each season.

In 1992 the Royal Society for the Protection of Birds bought Ramsey. There is now a resident warden on the island, who meets every visitor, though there are necessary restrictions on the number of people allowed on the island each day. For those lucky enough to make it, there are refreshments and a shop. Unpaid assistant wardens can arrange to stay and help with work on the reserve. To the south-west of Ramsey, quite a way out to sea, lies the RSPB's first Welsh island reserve - Grassholm.This small lump of rock is a National Nature Reserve and the breeding home to about 33,000 pairs of gannets. The island is a minimum of 6 miles from the mainland (depending on where you are coming from), but whether your journey is

Skomer in the spring

with the Thousand Islands boat (from Whitesands Bay) or the Dale Sailing boat (from Martin's Haven), the trip is well worth it, because Grassholm is the ultimate sight, sound and smell experience of the Pembrokeshire islands. It is also the second largest gannetry in the Northern Hemisphere. Landings on Grassholm are allowed only after 16th June.

Skomer

This is the largest of Pembrokeshire's islands, a National Nature Reserve owned by the Countryside Commission for Wales but run by Wales Wildlife Trust, who employ a permanent warden and staff.

The island ferry runs from Martin's Haven, on the Marloes Peninsula, every day except Monday, though during bank holidays the island is open to visitors all the time. There is a charge for the boat trip and also for landing, but children under 16 are exempt from the latter.

There are guided tours around Skomer, usually operated by the National Park Authority, but in the main visitors are greeted and given a brief informative talk, which includes information on where to find all the island's interesting sights and wildlife. From then until the boats leave in the afternoon, you are free to explore via the well-defined footpaths.

Skomer has some very well preserved archaeological remains dating back to the early Iron Age, in the form of standing stones, hut circles, burial cairns, walls and numerous lynchets. The island was farmed until the mid-1950's, but is now grazed only by rabbits - albeit 8-15,000 of them! The flora is not rich but the carpets of spring and early-summer flowering bluebells, red campion, white sea campion and thrift are some of the most colourful in the west.

The island's cliff scenery is spectacular, both scenically and for its many thousands of breeding guillemots, razorbills, kittiwakes and fulmars. More than 20,000 pairs of lesser black-backed gulls nest in the middle of the island - the largest colony of this species in Europe. Other gulls, such as greater black-backed and herring, are also well represented. Skomer, in fact, boasts the largest colony of breeding seabirds in southern Britain. This is in spite of many years' farming activity here, during which no species of ground predators - even rats or cats - ever managed to establish themselves. So ground and burrow nesting sites are numerous. There are over 6000 pairs of puffins and at least 165,000 pairs of Manx shearwaters - the world's biggest colony. Of the ground-nesting birds, there are good numbers of short-eared owls, curlews and oystercatchers, to name but a few.

Skomer is also home to a unique island race of bank voles, common shrews and wood mice, and on the beaches during the autumn over 150 grey seal pups are born, making this the second most important seal-breeding colony in south-western Britain. Another notable colony is that established by shags on Midland Island, a much smaller island south of Skomer.

Skomer, Grassholm and Skokholm are all included in a Special Protection Area designated by a European directive - a further indication of the value of Pembrokeshire's offshore islands to international wildlife.

A further attraction to visitors to Skomer is that the island has a limited amount of self-catering accommodation available. This is for paying holidaymakers and also for unpaid assistant wardens (6 people a week maximum), who help the warden with work on the reserve.

Skokholm

This small island (106 hectares) has been owned by the Dale Castle Estates since the 1970's and is now leased by Wales Wildlife Trust, who employ a cook and a warden. There is full-board accommodation for up to 16 people a week.

Skokholm has all the richness and profusion of wildlife and beauty of Skomer, but in a smaller, more gentle way. The only seabird not common to both is the kittiwake, and in the quarry on the westerly cliffs below the lighthouse there is a colony of several thousand storm petrels - the largest colony in the Irish Sea. In 1936 the island was set up as Britain's first ever bird observatory by a group of people which included Ronald (R.M.) Lockley. This, of course, is Lockley's Dream Island, which was occupied and farmed by him until 1940.

There are guided tours of Skokholm on every Monday between Whitsun and late August. The warden or his assistant act as guide, and the trips are booked through the National Park Authority.

St. Margaret's Island

St. Margaret's Island and its much bigger neighbour Caldey lie some way to the south of the county. St. Margaret's (another reserve of Wales Wildlife Trust) has the largest colony of cormorants in Wales, located on top of its steep limestone cliffs. Other seabirds here include greater black-backed and herring gulls in good numbers on top of the island, and guillemots, razorbills, kittiwakes and fulmars on the vertical cliffs. There are very few puffins, but burrow-nesting birds are restricted by the presence of rats. The island and its wildlife, and the coastline of Caldey, are best seen from one of the pleasure boats which run regularly from Tenby harbour between April and September. No landings are allowed on St. Margaret's.

Caldey

Caldey is owned and run by the small community of Cistercian monks, who farm the island with the help of the few people in the village.

A day out here is totally different from anything else you will experience in Pembrokeshire. Several boats a day take many curious visitors to this atmospheric and religious centre, and landings and access are simple compared to the islands already described.

If you leave the boat and walk towards the village and monastery, you pass Priory Beach - a beautiful, gently curving stretch of sand backed by dunes, and the island's only safe bathing beach. The easy stroll up through the trees (which are an exceptional feature on any offshore island) has a distinctly Mediterranean feel to it, which is emphasised when you see the monastery, overlooking the main village. The imposing but attractive monastic buildings are all whitewashed and have terra cotta roofs. The village itself has shops which include a perfumery, gift shop and cafe. The cafe serves tea, coffee, ice cream, yoghurt and chocolate, and the pleasant open-air seating is arranged under swaying, whispering trees.

Caldey

Thousand Islands Expeditions

The most novel and exciting way to see Pembrokeshire's islands!

Thousand Islands Expeditions, renowned for nearly a quarter of a century as offering one of the most exciting and rewarding ways to discover the world-famous Pembrokeshire islands, home to hundreds of thousands of seabirds and marine wildlife. We invite you to join one of our varied expeditions designed to suit everyone, young and old alike. Our expert staff will look after you very well and introduce you to a unique combination of adventure and sensitive appreciation of Pembrokeshire's myriad wildlife aboard our specially built, water-jet powered, rigid inflatable boats, famous for their reliability, safety and all-weather capabilities.

Alternatively, try our more traditional slow-boat voyages - we operate them all, from spectacular white-water jet-boat rafting over the 'Bitches of Ramsey Sound', or spending the day on Ramsey Island, visiting Grassholm Island and its' 100,000 nesting Gannets, Puffin watching, Dolphin watching, Whale watching and a whole lot more. Contact us now, adventures are easier with Thousand Islands Expeditions.

ALL INFORMATION CONTAINED HERE IS SUBJECT TO SEASONAL VARIATIONS, SEA CONDITIONS AND POLICY CHANGES.

INFORMATION & BOOKING OFFICE:

Cross Square, St. Davids, Pembrokeshire, SA62 6SL.

Tel: 01437 721686 Fax: 01437 720747

The Experience of a Lifetime

The Welsh Wildlife Centre

This unique wildlife experience is located just south of Cardigan and offers the visitor the opportunity to enjoy the wonders of the diverse wildlife of West Wales. The Centre, comprising of meadows, woodland, reed beds, marsh and riverside, is the home to some of Britain's most picturesque and exciting wildlife. This unique Centre houses some of the most endangered habitats where rare and fragile species are coming back from the brink of extinction. Red Kite, Cetti's Warbler, Marsh Harrier and the Little Egret are just some of the regular visitors to this nature reserve. The Centre is also the home to Otters and a wonderful display of rare wild flowers. Other countryside wildlife like Deer, Badgers, Shrews, Voles and Bats can also be seen in the seven different habitats on the reserve.

The Welsh Wildlife Centre offers weather-proof hides with seating for bird-watching at one of the UK's top bird-watching sites. The Visitor Centre includes a wildlife display and live micro camera links to an Otter Holt and Owl Nest Box for visitors, and also offers educational facilities for schools. The Centre includes a restaurant and gift shop and has all ability access for disabled visitors, unique conference facilities are also available. Special family super saver tickets and retired and disabled tickets are available. A full programme of events and activities for all ages runs throughout the season.

The Welsh Wildlife Centre is open from April to the end of October and, during the winter, the reserve is open at all times to enjoy the wonderful environment of the area. For further information telephone : 01239 621600, facsimile : 01239 613211. E-mail : wildlife@wildlife-wales.org.uk. Web site : www.wildlife-wales.org.uk.

Skomer Island

This Pembrokeshire island has one of the best sea bird and seal experiences in Southern Britain. The island is inhabited by Puffins, Guillemots, Razorbills,. Cormorants, Peregrines, Fulmar, Kittiwake and Short-eared Owls to name a few. Over half a million sea birds breed on Skomer throughout the year. The twentieth century has hardly touched this island, however, it is possible to take a look at Manx Shearwater in its underground home through a live TV link (over half the world's population breed on the island) - a world first. The diverse flora and fauna is set off by spectacular scenery on an island where the largest prehistoric Iron Age settlement in Britain can still be found.

Porpoise are often seen close-by to the island or can be one of your companions on the ferry to the island. Grey Seals can be seen all around the island and in September the seals give birth to their delightful pups.

Skokholm Island

This magnificent wildlife paradise is only half an hours boat trip from the mainland. It is a home to a wide variety of sea birds - tens of thousands of Puffin, Razorbill, Fulmar, Guillemot and, of course, the Manx Shearwater and Storm

Petrel, breed on this spectacular island and the wildlife experience is available to the public. The sea surrounding the island is the natural habitat for porpoise, dolphin and the occasional basking shark while grey seals bob round the many inlets

throughout the year.

Here you will find Britain's first bird observatory; established in the 1930's, and life remains as it was then.   Short-break or week long breaks (all full board) are available to experience the nocturnal return to the island of tens of thousands of Manx Shearwaters and Storm Petrels - this wildlife spectacle cannot be found anywhere else in the world.

There is also accommodation available on Skomer, both of which are run by the Wildlife Trust West Wales and for further information on this self-catering accommodation and full board on Skokholm, telephone : 01437 765462.

For further information see page 132 and Dale Sailing advert on page 133. Boats leave Martinshaven daily for the short crossing to the island. For further information on Skomer see page 133 in this guide.

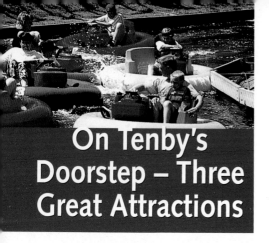

On Tenby's Doorstep – Three Great Attractions

The Tenby area is particularly well endowed with visitor attractions, and here we put the spotlight on three highly popular venues which are all within very easy driving distance of West Wales' premier seaside town.

Heatherton Country Sports Park, St. Florence

From the moment you arrive at Heatherton you will experience non-stop fun and adventure. Karting, Paintballing, Horse Riding, Golf, Pistol Shooting, Archery and Bumper Boat Racing are just some of the activities you can combine to fill your days out with action and adventure. Heatherton has become one of Wales' Premier tourist attractions with its unique blend of activities. And know to ensure that a day at the park gets better and better, introduced in 1999 was the Heatherton Paintball Experience & Heatherton Riding Centre.

Paintball Experience is guaranteed to get the adrenaline pumping and your hair standing on end as you experience armed combat through testing countryside. You will be given many tough tasks in varying challenging terrain. You could find yourself defending forts and huts, hiding in bunkers and tunnels, or planning an offensive through streams and trenches. If you are up to the challenge you may be able to capture a village, kidnap the president, plant a bomb etc. This activity is suitable for both groups and individuals, and all the latest equipment is provided. All you need to bring with you is a desire to have a great day out.

If you's prefer to witness some of Pembrokeshire's most picturesque countryside in a more tranquil surrounding Heatherton Riding Centre will be ideal for you. Whether you are experienced or a complete beginner there will be a horse or pony suitable for you. You can choose from 1 hour, 1½ hours or half day treks. If you require some instruction the outdoor arena is ideal to brush up on your technique. You will be provided with boots and hats, and will be under the expert supervision of our friendly staff. Heatherton is also home to Karting World - Wales' most exciting karting experience. Senior karts are capable of up to 50 mph and are the nearest most of us will get to Formula One racing with hair raising speed and exhilaration through chicanes and hair-pin bends. Junior karts are suitable for all ages, for the budding Damon Hill of the future. The karts can be booked for either a fun ride or for a race meeting between friends. Grand Prix group competitions can also be organised.

For the smallest members of the family the fun is unlimited at Indiana's Indoor Softplay Adventure Area. There is both a toddler area and an adventure area incorporating Slides, Ball Pools, Indoor Karts, Biff Bash, Ariel Runway, Motion

Heatherton

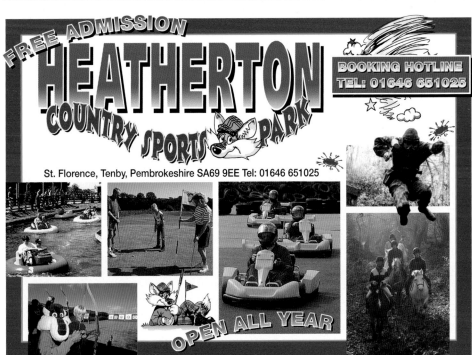

Sphere and Spooky Maze - all set in a jungle theme. This will ensure that the little ones have fun in safety, giving the parents a much deserved rest. There is seating available for the parents so that you can relax in the knowledge that all staff are fully qualified and the latest electronic tagging system will be in operation. You could then leave your children under expert supervision while you try some of the many other activities available.

The thrills of the Wild West can be enjoyed at Big H Pistol Shooting Range, you can find out who has the best reflexes at Laser Clay Pigeon Shooting or learn the skills of Archery under the supervision of our expert staff.

Join the Heatherton Hurricanes at Europe's only Baseball/Softball Range. This gives you the chance to hit a home run or get struck out. Choose between a Baseball or a Softball and you can also set the speed of the ball pitched to suit your hitting ability. Again, all equipment is provided.

For the aspiring golfer there is a challenging 18 hole Pitch and Putt course. With pond, stream, trees and bunkers, this par 3-4 course is ideal for the experienced or the beginner. The course is approximately 2,000 yards long, set in Pembrokeshire's beautiful countryside and is enjoyed by families and golfers alike. A 16 bay Golf Driving Range compliments the course.

Should you need to cool down you could have a splashing good time at the Bumper Boat Racing Lake. You can collide in safety at speeds of up to 14mph, and soak your friends at the same time!

Replace your lost energy at McFreddy's Fast Food Restaurant. Here you can sample all your favourite burgers, fries and light snacks. Alternatively you could visit the Outdoor Barbecue and Picnic Area to catch a breath between the non-stop action and adventure.

There is no entrance fee to the park -

Folly Farm

you simply pay and play, mix the activities which suit you, or choose to spend a day with our discount day-ticket. Heatherton is situated between Tenby and St.Florence with ample parking space.

So why wait to enjoy a day to remember! The whole family is guaranteed to enjoy your wildest day out in Wales.

Folly Farm - Wales' Premier Family Attraction

Head north from Tenby on the A478 towards Narberth and you will soon find this top family attraction, less than a mile from the roundabout at Kilgetty.

Folly Farm has a wide variety of attractions that appeal to all ages, ranging from farm activities to the thrills of the funfair.

Daily entertainment provides a fun-packed day for the whole family. For many guests, the highlight is the twice daily opportunity to bottle-feed the farm's younger animals in the covered all-weather Jolly Barn. Watch the herd of cows being milked and try your hand at milking a goat, or one of the farm's friendly cows under the expert guidance of a Folly Farmer. Meet many more animals when you visit Percy's Piggery, the Horses' Hideout and the Pet Centre.

Don't miss an awe-inspiring display which is provided twice daily by the birds of prey, with the resident falconer demonstrating how these fascinating hunters use all their natural instincts.

Special events take place throughout the season, from the Easter Extravaganza to Summer Entertainment Days, ensuring that the whole family are entertained.

Travel back in time and enjoy Folly Farm's Vintage Fun Fair. An undercover centre that enables you to rekindle the spirit and nostalgic atmosphere of yesteryear. Reminiscent of the annual fairs that took place in Pembrokeshire up until the early part of the century, this is one of the largest working collections of popular rides. Included are the waltzer, ghost train, swingboats, chair-o-planes, the 1937 royal coronation speedway and the 1922 gallopers, all set among stalls and antique farm machinery. New attractions for 2000 include original dodgem and swirl rides.

Great fun for budding and experienced drivers alike are the Formula 2 go -karts. These exhilarating karts can accommodate a small child with accompanying adult.

From life in the fast lane, guests can take advantage of the relaxing countryside walks. Regular tractor and trailer rides will transport you to and from the nature trail which meanders through the lovely Pembrokeshire landscape.

Folly Farm has plenty to offer including restaurants, burger bar, the Dog & Duck licensed bar, gift shops and much, much more. At Folly Farm, the fun never stops, regardless of the weather, be sure to call for more information on 01834 812731 or why not check out our website at www.folly-farm.co.uk

Oakwood

A Millennium family cracker is waiting to go bang at Wales' premier theme park as it opens its gates on a new century this April 15th!

A host of New Year surprises are waiting to be unveiled at Oakwood Park in Pembrokeshire - including a heart-thumping attraction for thrill-seekers, extra special fun for little 'uns and an entertainment extravaganza for all the family during the Easter holidays. Plus Oakwood's already renowned stable of white-knuckle and thrill family rides set at the heart of some of Pembrokeshire's prettiest coastal countryside.

To celebrate the New Millennium, Oakwood is hosting its own Mardi Gras style party in New Orleans - where the music goes on all day, whatever the weather! For two weeks only at Easter, you can sit out at an undercover street cafe in the French Quarter and enjoy the unique flavour of the Deep South, live blues and jazz bands, speciality coffees, aperitifs and special New Orleans cuisine. Whatever you do, you'll be singing away those blues! The Mardis Gras magic ends each evening with a spectacular night-time light parade boasting ten illuminated floats! But don't get too comfortable - there is a spine-tingling surprise waiting to be discovered right in the heart of New Orleans!

For younger children, there are more surprises in store! Playtown is already a firm favourite for little ones - a capital city of delight where children are free to pilot their own jet, captain their own mini-Pirate Ship, head for the high roads in their own Truck Convey, reach for the skies in the mini-Ferris Wheel or conquer the tiniest rollercoaster in the west with a terrifying first drop of 3ft and a dizzy top speed of 6mph - a training ground for future coaster nuts! But there is a whole new undercover world of fun to come - and kids will feel like giants in this special playland built just for them!

As it opens for its thirteenth season, good fortune is still smiling on this hugely popular Welsh tourist attraction which now welcomes some 450,000 visitors every year.

Last year, Oakwood blasted to success with its new white-knuckle ride - the UK's first 47m high Shot 'n Drop tower coaster The Bounce which shoots riders into the air at speeds of 70 kph and 4 G-force in less than two seconds only to freefall back to ground - and then 'bounce' back up again!

The Bounce joined Oakwood's growing stable of award-winning rides: the ultimate wooden rollercoaster Megafobia, voted best in the world for four consecutive years; Vertigo, a 50m skycoaster that soars at speeds of up to 110 kph in 1.5 seconds and described as the closest sensation to free flight imaginable; Europe's largest watercoaster Snake River Falls.

These internationally-acclaimed rides are set amidst other all-time family favourites - The Pirate Ship, Treetops Coaster, The Waterfall, The Bobsleigh, Go-Karts, the Boating Lake and the Skyleap - a glittering array of more than forty fun rides and attractions for all the family.

During Oakwood's Late Night Opening Season in August, the park stays open until 10pm and bravehearts who come during the day can stay After Dark for free to enjoy Oakwood's spectacular summer showtime season. Evening visitors arriving after 5.30pm can join the party at a special price. The After Dark entertainment programme includes two fully-themed entertainment venues and the evening ends with a bang with one of Wales' most spectacular fireworks displays and waterscreen lightshow.

In December, Oakwood opens its gates on the fairytale Magical Christmasland, The North Pole and popular family pantomime. Here, families can be whisked away to Santa's own winter wonderland home in the heart of west Wales, meet his animated elves

Megafobia: Europe's largest wooden rollercoaster

in Santa's Magical Workshop, sing-along with Rudolph the singing reindeer and Frosty the Snowman and play in 13,000 square feet of arctic adventure playland and themed games. All rounded off with a legendary trip to the colourful world of traditional vaudeville in Oakwood's Magical Theatre.

Near to the theme park is CC2000, the an interactive family entertainment centre for all the family. The centre is home to the popular Channel Four Adventure Game The Crystal Maze, a ten-lane BTBA approved bowling alley and Games Sector One, a fully-themed amusement centre based on a surreal spaceship design and featuring the most technologically advanced high realism simulators, video and games machines. After the fun, simply relax in the fully-licensed bar and cafeteria - the ultimate day out.

All in all, there is Millennium magic for all the family at Oakwood Park in the Year 2000 - so make sure you're there on April 15th to enjoy it!

145

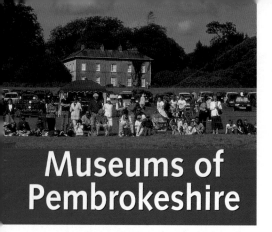

Museums of Pembrokeshire

Scolton Manor

Scolton House is a fine example of a Victorian country house. In recent years the period rooms on three floors have been carefully restored in a late Victorian style, similar to how the house may have looked at the turn of the century. The lived-in atmosphere portrays life 'above and below stairs'.

In addition to the period rooms, two exhibition galleries have also been developed in the house. The Art Gallery features varied exhibitions of fine art and photographs organised by the Arts Officer. The Costume Gallery has the intriguing title - Victorian Vogue: the Manor and the Military. Using items from the county's costume collection, the gallery tells the story of the development of Victorian costume appropriate to those 'at home' on a country estate like Scolton. The display also includes some wonderful military uniforms including a selection from the Pembroke Yeomanry Collection.

Developments in the original Stable Buildings illustrate what life was like on a Pembrokeshire country estate - stabling for horses, a complete carpenter's workshop and a blacksmith's forge, skills once so important to life in the past but now almost forgotten. Background sound effects help to bring the displays alive.

The Railway Area beyond the Stable Complex focuses on Margaret, the oldest remaining GWR 0-6-0 saddle-tank locomotive in Britain, which ran on the Maenclochog Railway between 1878 and 1904. This locomotive and the signal box from Sarnau, Bancyfelin, and an exhibition adjacent to the railway area, tell the complete story of railways in Pembrokeshire and also much about the industries of the County in the early 20th century. Sound effects, lit railway lamps, an interactive computer quiz and a coin-operated Hornby train attract people of all ages. Inside the gallery is a restored Wickham Trolley made in 1942 which spent part of its working life with the Great Western Railway at Milford Haven transporting railwaymen along the track. The gallery also contains over a hundred rare photographs, many of which are available for sale from the museum by arrangement.

The Exhibition Hall contains many exciting and new displays. The centerpiece is 'The Field' - a display of the museum's agricultural collection, a permanent reminder of the importance of farming to the County of Pembrokeshire. On a somewhat different theme the 'World War II: Homefront Gallery' includes an Anderson shelter and a piece of the famous prototype bouncing bomb designed by Barnes Wallace. On the first floor, visitors can view the Prehistory of Pembrokeshire Gallery, as well as the constantly changing display of the finds of the Pembrokeshire Prospectus Society. Also on this level is the museum's newest development 'Peoples Gallery'. This gallery is filled with the collections of local people from corn dollies to computers!

The collections at Scolton include fine and decorative art, social and industrial history, costume, military history, archaeology, geology and natural history. Information on the history of Pembrokeshire, local industries and the Scolton estate is available for teachers,

Pembrokeshire Museums Association

Tenby Museum & Art Gallery

Castle Hill, Tenby, Pembrokeshire SA70 7BP
Tel/Fax: (01834) 842809
EASTER- OCTOBER:
Every day 10.00am - 5.00pm
NOVEMBER- EASTER:
Mondays to Fridays 10.00am - 5.00pm
Admission Charges
Concessions and family tickets
Research facilities: library and archives:
by appointment
Museum Shop www.atlas-links.com

The Wilson Museum of Narberth

AMGUEDDFA WILSON YN ARBERTH
Market Square, Narberth, Pembrokeshire SA67 7AU
Tel: (01834) 861719
Monday to Friday 10.30am - 5.00pm, Saturday 10.30am -
12.30pm from Easter Saturday until the last Saturday in
September. At other times by appointment
Office and shop open all the year round
Research facilities available by appointment
Admission Charges with the usual concessions
Friends of the Museum and childnen under 12 - FREE
School parties by prior arrangement - FREE

County Contrasts Follow the Museum Trail
Haverfordwest . Medieval County Town
Milford Haven. Pembrokeshire'New' Town
Narberth . Old Market Town
Scolton Manor · Pembrokeshire Country Museum
Tenby · Medieval Walled Town
Visit these five fascinating Museums
Members of the Pembrokeshire Museums Association

The Milford Haven Museum

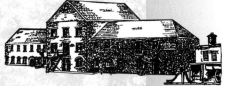

The Old Custom House, The Docks,
Milford Haven, Pembrokeshire SA73 3AF
Tel: (01646) 694496
EASTER- OCTOBER:
Monday to Saturday 11.00am - 5.00pm
Sunday opening 12.00noon - 6.00pm
on bank holidays and school holidays
Parties accommodated at anytime, by appointment
Admission Charges and concessions

Haverfordwest Town Museum

Castle House, Haverfordwest Castle,
Haverfordwest, Pembrokeshire
Tel (01437) 763087
EASTER - OCTOBER:
Mondays to Saturdays 10.00am -4.00pm
Admission Charges, Concessions and Family Tickets

Scolton Manor Museum

Spittal, Haverfordwest, Pembrokeshire SA62 SQL
Tel: (01437) 731328 Fax: (01437) 731743
The museum is 5 miles from Haverfordwest on
the B4329 Cardigan road.
APRIL - OCTOBER:
Tuesday to Sunday 10.30am - 5.30pm
Also open Bank Holidays within the season
Admission Charge for Adults
Reduction for children
Adult ticket concessions available
Research facilities available by appointment

school parties and researchers. Guided tours can be arranged by prior booking. Museum staff can assist with identifying objects and there is a library facility for interested people to do local studies research.

The museum shop stocks a varied range of interesting postcards, booklets and souvenirs relating to the heritage of Pembrokeshire.

Penrhos Cottage

This cottage is a typical north Pembrokeshire thatched cottage which has survived almost unchanged since the 19th century. It was first built as a ty unnos or overnight cottage in about 1800 and later rebuilt in stone. Penrhos provides a unique opportunity to view the cottager's life in the past as it has its original Welsh oak furniture.

Penrhos Cottage is open by appointment. For further details contact Scolton Manor Museum.

Tenby Museum & Art Gallery

The award-winning community museum is one of Tenby's best known attractions, with the reputation of being one of the finest independent museums in the country. It has occupied a spectacular site on Castle Hill overlooking Caldey Island since 1878.

The museum is a pleasant place for all ages to explore and many come every year to see the changing displays. The galleries show how the archaeology and geology of Pembrokeshire, its natural history, maritime and social history: tracing the aspects of Tenby's social development up to the present day. The local history gallery features special temporary exhibitions on

Penrhos Cottage

Tenby Museum

the history of Tenby and South Pembrokeshire. The museum publishes several books and factsheets on aspects of local history and works closely with a number of schools and colleges.

The art gallery is an especially important feature: for many, it is the main purpose of their visit. The collection contains several works by local artists such as Augustus John and Gwen John, both of whom have attained international reputations and are among the few eminent Welsh artists of the Twentieth Century. The collection also contains work by another local artist, Nina Hamnett - an "English Modern" painter. There is a significant collection of the work of the local early nineteenth century topographical artist Charles Norris.

There are additional images from the eighteenth century onwards by artists who have visited and been inspired by the beauty of the area, such as H.G Gasineau, J.C Ibbetson and W.P Frith.

The museum provides a wide range of gifts including books, prints, posters, cards and other items of relevance to the museum's collections.

The Museum & Art Gallery is open daily between Easter and the end of October (10am to 5pm) and Monday to Friday only from November to Easter (10am to 5pm). The extensive library and archive collections may be consulted for research purposes by appointment.

Milford Haven Museum

Milford Haven Museum brings to life the fascinating story of the historic waterway and a new town's struggle to fulfil its potential.

Lying on the north shore os one of the best natural harbours in the world, Milford Haven is barely 200 years old. It was first settled in 1790 by tough, independent Quaker whalemen from Nantucket Island in America. They helped plan and lay out the town under the direction of the Frenchmen Jean Louis Barrallier. The museum is housed in one of their earliest buildings.

The Milford Haven Story is a cycle of hopes dashed and dreams unfulfilled. Its brief period as a whaling port ended when coal gas replaced whale oil for lighting the streets of London. Its attempt to become a great Trans-Atlantic Port floundered when the G.W.R terminus was placed at Neyland and not Milford.

Prosperity as a major fishing port from 1888 to the late 1950's came as a second option. The fishing industry attracted people from all over the British Isles: herring fishers from the east coast and Scotland, fishermen from the south west and the east coast, engineers from Scotland and the north east.

They and their descendants and those who came with the oil refineries in the mid/late 1900's make Milford Haven one of the most cosmopolitan towns in the U.K.

Haverfordwest Town Museum

Haverfordwest is the county town of Pembrokeshire and has been established for almost 1000 years. It was the main port in West Wales until the coming of the railway. The castle is in the centre of the town and dominates it.

The museum has been created recently to illustrate the history of the castle and the town. It is situated in the castle itself, along with the County Record Office. It contains exhibits explaining the castle and prison, transport and industry in the town

and the institutions and personalities of the town.

It has an interactive multimedia computer which is easy for visitors to use and is packed with information and photographs of the town.

Car parking is available in the castle grounds. Drive through the town around one way system. Turn RIGHT by Bethesda Chapel into Queen's Square (Church Street). Castle entrance is at the top of the hill.

The Wilson Museum, Narberth

Narberth is a small town with a long history. It is mentioned as Arberth in the collection of ancient Welsh stories known as the Mabinogi. It boasts a 12th-century castle and a 13th-century church, but it was its position on the cattle drovers' route from the far west of Wales that helped by the beginning of the 20th-century, to make it a prosperous centre with a weekly market, eight annual cattle fairs, a flourishing newspaper and over twenty public houses.

The Wilson Museum, situated in the office of James Williams, a 19th-century wine and spirit merchant, has a rich collection of objects and photographs illustrating the life of Narberth's people and surrounding villages. It records their shops and businesses, their schools and choirs, their successes and failures from flying to photography, from printing to brewing. The paraphernalia of their personal lives is all here from dresses and hats, bibles and cookery books to toys and personal possessions, radios and ration books.

The Museum shop, which specialises in books on all aspects of Welsh culture, also stocks cards, small gifts, classical and Welsh CDs and tapes, books relating to the Museum's collections and children's books.

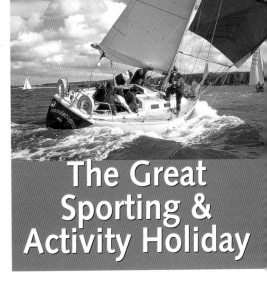

The Great Sporting & Activity Holiday

ealth and fitness are an increasingly important facet of modern lifestyles, and this is reflected in the growing number of visitors who come to Pembrokeshire in search of sporting and activity holidays.

Certainly, there is no better place to choose: with the only coastline in Britain to be designated a national park, and many well-established sporting attractions already here, Pembrokeshire combines the best of the great outdoors with the very best in indoor leisure facilities - as the following guide illustrates.

Adventure & Exploration

St. David's Adventure Days : For more information ring 01437 721611 or freephone 0800 132588

Thousand Island Expeditions, St. David's : See page 138

Buggying

All-Terrain Vehicles, Ritec Valley Buggies, Penally : Ring 01834 843390.

Canoeing

West Wales Windsurfing, Sailing & Canoeing, Dale : See under Watersports.

Climbing

Pembrokeshire offers climbers of all abilities the opportunity to experience some of the finest sea-cliff climbing in the British Isles. The county's geographic location and mild winters mean all-year-round climbing on dry, warm rock - a treat rarely available in mountainous areas. So the area is very popular, especially during early bank holidays, and there may well be queues for some of the plum 3-star routes.

The sea cliffs are the home of many nesting birds, some of them rare, and because of this there are very necessary restrictions in certain areas from early February to mid-August. So choose your routes carefully. It cannot be stressed too strongly that if climbers and wildlife are to co-exist successfully in this environmentally sensitive corner of Britain, the restrictions imposed must be adhered to. Further details of these restrictions are available from all National Park Information Centres in the county, and in the Climber's Guide to Pembrokeshire.

You should also remember that this hazardous coastline keeps the coastguard and rescue services fully occupied without any further help from stranded climbers. So at all times take every possible safety precaution, including the use of a helmet because of the ever-present danger of loose rock.

Coasteering

Preseli Outdoor Centre, Mathry : See under Kayaking on page 158.

Country Sports

Heatherton Country Sports Park, St. Florence See page 140

Cycling & Mountain Biking

There is no better way to enjoy the magnificence of the Pembrokeshire coastline and the beauty and tranquillity of the countryside than on a mountain bike - especially as the whole of the National Park is criss-crossed with a network of hidden tracks, bridle ways and sunken lanes. When cycling in Pembrokeshire it is very important to remember that the coast path is for walkers only - a law strictly enforced by the National Park Authority, who are responsible for maintaining this long-distance footpath. Furthermore, off-road cyclists should at all times give way to walkers and horse riders, and be courteous and considerate to the farmers and landowners whose land they are crossing.

For cyclists who prefer to be on the road than off it, Pembrokeshire has more quiet lanes than most people could cycle round in a lifetime. Touring in the county could hardly be easier, with bed and breakfast available round every corner and plenty of youth hostels within easy reach. And there's even more help and encouragement on hand at Mike's Bikes in Haverfordwest. Proprietor Mike Evans is himself a very keen cyclist and a member of the Cyclists Touring Club. Visitors to the area are particularly welcome to call into his shop for advice on local routes, from 5 miles to 50 miles.

Gwaun Valley Mountain Bikes, Cilgwyn, near Newport: Ring 01239 820905.

Haven Sports, Broad Haven: Mountain biking is one of several sports

available here. For more information see under Watersports.

Mike's Bikes, Haverfordwest: This specialist cycle shop caters for the whole family, offering a comprehensive range of bikes, clothing and accessories, plus advice on local routes. Services include cycle hire, repairs carried out on the premises and free delivery of new bikes for customers within a 30-mile radius. For more information ring 01437 760068.

Preseli Mountain Bikes, Mathry: Ring 01348 837709.

Fishing

Whether you are looking for an out-and-out fishing holiday or you simply want to enjoy a bit of fishing while you're here, Pembrokeshire and West Wales provide wonderful opportunities for sea, game and coarse fishing.

The coastlines of Pembrokeshire, Cardigan Bay and Carmarthen Bay are excellent venues for summer sea angling, either from beaches or from established rock marks. Bass, pollack, garfish, mackerel, conger eel and even tope are all here for the taking. And if you want to fish offshore, there is no shortage of charter boats offering fishing trips from local harbours.

West Wales has long been renowned for the quality of its game fishing, with most of the area's rivers and their tributaries experiencing good runs of salmon and sea trout during the summer months. Indeed, the region boasts three of Britain's premier salmon rivers - the Towy, Teifi and Taf and many others provide terrific sport when conditions are favourable. These include the Nevern, Aeron, Eastern Cleddau, Western Cleddau, Rheidol and Ystwyth.Wales also has an abundance of lakes and reservoirs which are well stocked with brown and rainbow trout. Venues popular with visitors are the reservoirs at Llys-y-fran Country Park and Rosebush (both close to the B4329, about 6 miles northeast of Haverfordwest), White House Mill and Latch y Goroff (near Whitland), and the trout fisheries of Llwyndrissi, Llanllawddog and Garnffrwd (near Carmarthen).

For coarse anglers, there are exciting prospects at a variety of locations. Bosherston lakes offer excellent pike fishing, and Llyn Carfan lake at Tavernspite, between Red Roses and Whitland, boasts top-class carp fishing and a good head of tench and roach. Glas Llyn fishery near Blaenwaen is also stocked with carp and tench.

Anybody aged 12 or over who fishes for salmon, trout, freshwater fish or eels in England and Wales must have an Environment Agency rod fishing licence, available from the Post Office or Environment Agency offices. In addition, you must have permission of the fishery

153

owner before you may fish on waters under his or her control. And remember, take your litter home, as discarded tackle can injure wildlife.

Puddleduck Trout Fishery: Situated in a beautiful woodland setting on the Haverfordwest-Burton road near Freystrop, lies Puddleduck Trout Fishery - a recently established fly fishery owned by Graham and Jenny Roach.

This lovely attraction has two well stocked lakes totalling nearly four acres and also boasts a log cabin pavilion which accommodates a rest room, a tackle shop, toilet facilities, and light refreshments. There is ample parking and the fishery is open all year from 8am to dusk. For more information you can contact Puddleduck on 01437 891845.

Llys-y-fran Reservoir & Country Park, near Rosebush: See page 108.

Flying
Haverfordwest School of Flying and Microlight Centre: Ring 01437 760822.

Golf
Serious golfers (don't forget your handicap certificate!) have plenty to tax their skills in Pembrokeshire, with a choice of challenging courses to play.

At Tenby there is a superb 18-hole links course which regularly hosts events such as the Welsh National Championships, and in Pembroke Dock the hillside course of South Pembrokeshire Golf Club, which enjoys panoramic views over the Haven, has now been developed into an 18-hole course.

On the other side of the waterway are the two first-class 18-hole courses at Haverfordwest and Milford Haven. In the north of the county, the golf clubs of St. David's and Newport both have 9-hole

links courses, and Newport offers the added attraction of self-catering holiday flats adjoining the clubhouse.

Haverfordwest Golf Club
The club was formed in 1904, but it was not until 1983 that the course was extended to its present 18 holes. The new clubhouse and has excellent facilities, including two bars. There are also changing rooms, showers and a pro shop. For more information ring 01437 763565.

Mayfield Golf Range, Freystrop, near Haverfordwest: Ring 01437 764300.

Milford Haven Golf Club: Ring 01646 692368.

Milford Marina Golf Course: Ring 01646 692272.

Newport Golf Club & Dormy House Holiday Flats: Here you have a golf course which overlooks the magnificent coastline of Newport Bay, and superbly appointed holiday flats which overlook both! The interesting 9-hole par 35 links course is a challenge to players of all standards. The clubhouse offers full catering facilities, and the self-catering flats adjoin the clubhouse and sleep up to 4 people. For more information ring 01239 820244.

Newport

Priskilly Forest Golf Club, Letterston, Near Fishguard: For more information ring 01348 840276.

St. David's City Golf Club: Established in 1902, this is one of the oldest golf clubs in Wales, and certainly the most westerly. And this is no fair-weather course, because all 9 holes stand on the sand dunes which back beautiful Whitesands Bay - so conditions underfoot are always dry and the course is playable all year round. With the added attraction of stunning views over the bay and St. David's Head, it is not surprising that this 6000-yard par 70 course is so popular with visitors. For more information ring the clubhouse on 01437 721751 or the secretary on 01437 720312.

South Pembrokeshire Golf Club: The club is beautifully located overlooking the Haven waterway. The course has now been extended from 9 to 18 holes, and there is also a new clubhouse, where you can enjoy a warm Pembrokeshire welcome in the bar and dining room. The club is only five minutes' drive from the Irish Ferries terminal at Pembroke Dock. For more information ring 01646 621453.

Tenby Golf Club : The oldest course in Wales with first class clubhouse facilities. 18 holes. Ring 01834 842787.

Trefloyne Golf Course

Now in its fourth year since opening for play in June 1996, Trefloyne Golf Course continues to enhance its reputation as a premier parkland course.

The careful integration of natural features and hazards during construction, coupled with a regimen of meticulous maintenance from tee to green, has ensured a marvellous combination of tough par 3s, exciting par 4s and formidable par 5s. All who take up the challenge offered by this beautiful 6635 yard, Par 71, 18 hole course, not only experience the delight of playing within an idyllic parkland landscape with superb views over Carmarthen Bay and Caldey Island, but also find their golfing skills well and truly tested.

For further information ring Steven Laidler on 01834 842165, or, visit our Internet web site at http://www.fhgilman.co.uk/html/golf

Horse Riding

With its lush countryside, quiet lanes, bridle paths and spectacular beaches, Pembrokeshire has the ideal environment for riding, which has long been a very popular leisure pursuit all over the county. There are a number of riding stables catering for visitors, and you can even book a riding or pony trekking holiday. And if you prefer spectating to being in the saddle, there are many events and shows to see, including gymkhanas, show jumping and point-to-point.

Horse Riding in the Landsker Borderlands

The Dunes Riding Centre, Martletwy

The stables are located south of Narberth only 800yards from Oakwood Park. With rides to suit all abilities from a half hour for the under 5's to a full day for the really experienced through woodland and along quiet lanes, The Dunes Riding Centre specialise in making your value for money riding break really enjoyable. New for the Millennium is our One-2-One Pony Experience for children over 8 years with some experience - a day of riding and pony care! Riding hats and footware are supplied at no extra charge and all rides are accompanied by our cheerful and competent escorts. Nervous adults and children can be led if required. For more information or to book, telephone 01834 891398, fax 01834 891473, or e-mail mike@dunes-riding.fsnet.co.uk

East Tarr Riding Stables, St. Florence: Ring 01834 871274.

Norchard Farm Riding School, Manorbier: Everyone is catered for here - child or adult, beginner or experienced rider - with horses and ponies to suit all ages and abilities. There are organised daily rides and treks through farmland, hills and quiet lanes and tracks. Riding hats are provided. A qualified BHS instructor is available for lessons and jumping tuition. For more information ring 01834 871242.

Plumstone Trekking Centre : Located at the foot of Plumstone Mountain, just over 5 miles north of Haverfordwest on the B4330 towards Hayscastle Cross, this new trekking centre is open all year round. Based in a glorious countryside setting at Prescelly View Farm, the family-run Centre caters for riders and beginners of all ages and abilities and is fully licensed. The Centre is within very easy reach of Haverfordwest, Fishguard and St. David's. For more information ring 01437 741536.

Karting

BP Karting, Withybush Showground, Haverfordwest.

Why not try something different! Experience the thrills of karting in a safe and controlled environment where trained marshalls are always on hand to give help and advice. The Karts themselves have full racing chassis, slick tyres and are powered by Honda GX160 engines governed to give a top speed of approximately 35mph. Each kart is linked to a computer and laps are continually monitored. On completeion you will receive a personal print-out of your lap times and of course crash helmets and overalls are provided free for all drivers. Bookings for individual drivers are not necessary - just arrive and drive! BP Karting is open 7 days a week from 10 am till 10 pm during the holiday periods. For more information phone 01437 769555

Kayaking

North Pembrokeshire's dramatic coastline offers just the sort of conditions ideal for kayaking. For beginners there are quiet sheltered bays where even the complete novice soon feels at home, while the more expert can take up the challenge of tide races and overfalls. Beginners are often surprised to discover that even on their first trip, under the guidance of an experienced and qualified instructor, they begin to master the basic skills and are able to enjoy the thrills of exploring cliffs and sea caves and negotiating rocks and waves.

Another growing sport is coasteering. Definitely an activity for the more daring, this involves a combination of climbing and scrambling along the rocky coastline, swimming and cliff jumping.

Preseli Outdoor Centre, Mathry
Expert tuition in kayaking is offered

here, plus 2-day and 3-day BCU courses at all levels, as well as the chance to try your hand at coasteering - another sport which is rapidly gaining ground in the popularity stakes. For more information ring 01348 837709.

Pembrokeshire County Council - Sports & Leisure Centres

Sports centres are located in most of the larger towns throughout the county and boast an impressive array of facilities.

Fishguard Sports Centre

The Centre is located within the local high school, with whom it shares the facilities. These include a 20-metre swimming pool, sunbed, tennis courts, sports hall with 4 badminton courts, and a fitness suite and sauna. The Centre runs a variety of courses and a full junior holiday programme. For more information ring 01348 874514.

Haverfordwest Sports Centre

This is situated on the Sir Thomas Picton School site and comprises a 4-court badminton main hall, 2 squash courts, a fully-equipped Pulsestar fitness suite, football pitches and a recently-constructed full-size floodlit astro-grass pitch, which was sponsored by Sportslot, Foundation of Sport and Art and Pembrokeshire County Council. The Centre specialises in holiday courses for young people - so school holidays need never be boring! Summer play schemes provide for the under-8's, and the Centre is registered with Social Services. Whatever your sporting needs, ring 01437 765901 after 3.30pm for further information.

Meads Sports & Leisure Centre, Milford Haven

The extent of the facilities and variety of activities available here are impressive by any standards. The sports hall hosts badminton, 5-a-side football, volleyball, hockey, basketball, netball and many other sports, and the 25-metre swimming pool offers lessons for all ages, lifesaving classes, water polo, and facilities for those with special needs. There is also a purpose-built indoor bowls centre, sauna, solarium, fitness and recreation rooms, changing rooms for outdoor sports, refreshments, and courses in various sports and activities. The Centre also administers, and handles bookings for, the Thornton Hall Sports Centre (see separate entries).

For more information about Meads Sports & Leisure Centre ring 01646 694011.

Pembroke Leisure Centre

Facilities here include swimming pool, solarium, weight training and fitness room, table tennis, and courts for tennis, badminton and squash. You can also play 5-a-side football. The Centre is located next to Pembroke Comprehensive School between Pembroke and Pembroke Dock. For more information ring 01646 684434 or 683281.

Tenby Leisure Centre

Tenby's excellent new leisure centre boasts first-class indoor facilities: main swimming pool and learner pool (both with good access for disabled visitors); soft play area for children; health suite with Jacuzzi,

Newgale

steam room and sauna; solarium; fitness suite; dance and aerobics hall; main hall for badminton, table tennis, 5-a-side soccer, basketball and other games; cafe; and extensive free parking. For further information, ring 01834 843575.

Thornton Hall & Outdoor Sports Centre, Milford Haven School: Available during evenings and weekends, facilities include an indoor sports hall and a full-size floodlit soccer/hockey pitch with an artificial surface. Bookings must be made through the Meads Sports and Leisure Centre. For more information ring 01646 694011.

Quad Biking

Quad Trail Valley: Pembrokeshire's newest venture centre opened in June 1997 and is located near Letterston, just off the A40 on the road to Fishguard. The four-mile quad trail is set in the beautiful

Knox valley. Experienced instructors give confidence to even the most nervous of riders. The trail is open to all above the age 14 and reductions are given for groups of four or more. All the necessary safety helmets and wet-weather gear are included in the ticket price. For further information ring 01348 840676.

Sailing

Traditionally, dinghy sailing is very popular all over Pembrokeshire and southwest Wales. Yacht clubs such as Newport, Fishguard and Solva in the north of the county, and Tenby and Saundersfoot in the south, offer a friendly club atmosphere and a variety of facilities and racing programmes. Along the Milford Haven waterway - perhaps the most popular sailing location because it is sheltered from the open sea - you will find some of the larger and more active clubs, such as Neyland, Pembroke Haven, Pembrokeshire (Gelliswick, Milford Haven), and Dale.

For dinghy-sailing tuition, Dale is a location difficult to beat. West Wales Windsurfing, Sailing and Canoeing, who are based at Dale and officially recognised by the Royal Yachting Association, offer residential and non-residential courses at all levels and of the highest quality, including catamaran sailing. Dinghy hire is also available from them.

For yachtsmen, the Haven has 22 miles of navigable inland waterway, with the additional challenge of exciting offshore sailing to the nearby islands of Skomer, Skokholm and Grassholm.

The Haven has newly-built marinas at Milford Haven and Neyland, new pontoons at Dale, Angle, Burton and Neyland, and various mooring sites all along the waterway.

Dale Yacht Club: Ring 01646 636362.

Milford Marina: Ring 01646 692272.

Neyland Marina: Ring 01646 601601.

Pembrokeshire Yacht Club, Gelliswick, Milford Haven: Ring 01646 692799 or 692953.

West Wales Windsurfing, Sailing & Canoeing, Dale: See under Watersports.

Surfing

Big waves, clear blue unpolluted waters, no crowds, and relatively mild air and water temperatures - the tempting combination which Pembrokeshire offers to surfers who are willing to travel that little bit further in order to stand out from the rest. Late summer and early autumn are particularly good times to take advantage of the county's superb beaches and surfing conditions.

Freshwater West, in South Pembrokeshire, boasts the biggest and most consistent waves in the whole of Wales, with a variety of breaks to choose from. However, there are strong currents and no lifeguards, so beginners should not surf here. Other beaches worth checking out nearby include Broad Haven (south), Freshwater East and Manorbier. In North Pembrokeshire, good surfing can be enjoyed at Whitesands Bay, Newgale, Broad Haven and West Dale.

With the increasing popularity of surfing, more and more specialist shops are opening in the county, offering gear for hire and sale, along with information about the best locations. One of the better known outlets is Newsurf, situated right on the beach front at Newgale, while the outdoor centres at Twr-y-Felin, in St. David's, and West Wales Windsurfing, Dale, offer equipment and tuition.

Dale

Haven Sports, Broad Haven: See under Windsurfing.

Newsurf, Newgale: Located in Newgale Filling Station, Newsurf welcomes everyone interested in surfing and watersports - young and not so young, beginners and experts. There is a wide range of equipment for sale and hire, including surf skis, surfboards, body boards and wetsuits in all sizes. A changing room and hot shower are also available, along with a selection of surfing accessories and leisurewear. Newsurf is open 7 days a week and there are regular training sessions. For more information ring 01437 721398. For daily surf reports ring 01437 720698.

Swimming Pools

Fishguard Sports Centre: See page 158

Haverfordwest Swimming Pool: The pool celebrated its 25th anniversary in 1994, and the facilities it offers are now among the best in Wales. The superb million-pound complex includes the main 25-metre pool, which is maintained at a constant water temperature of 84_F and features Olympic springboards and a 92-foot water slide. The smaller and much shallower learner and hydrotherapy pool is underwater-lit and has special wheelchair access, with water maintained at a constant 93'F. In addition to the pools, the centre now boasts a well-equipped health club. Here you will find a private solarium suite, a steam room and sauna designed specially to suit wheelchairs as well as the able-bodied, power showering and massage, and relaxation loungers. For more information ring 01437 764354, 01437 765193 or 0800 600900.

Narberth Swimming Pool: Ring 01834 860940.

Tenby Leisure Centre: See under Leisure Centres.

Walking

Walks by the National Park Authority
From early April to the end of September, the Pembrokeshire Coast National Park Authority conducts an extensive programme of special activities and events for visitors, including guided walks. Details are published in the free newspaper, Coast to Coast.

Landsker Walking Festival: For more information ring SPARC on 01834 860965.

Pembrokeshire Coastal Path
There are many excellent guides to the 186-mile coast path. You can also obtain information and advice from any National Park Information Centre.

Watersports

Llys-y-fran Reservoir & Country Park, near Rosebush: See page 108

Pembrokeshire Watersports Project, Pembroke Dock: A variety of courses and opportunities including dinghy sailing, canoeing, powerboating and other water-sports are on offer through this new initiative. For further information ring 01646 622013.

West Wales Windsurfing, Sailing & Canoeing, Dale: One of Britain's leading water-sports centres, and approved by the Royal Yachting Association and the Wales Tourist Board, this is definitely the place to come to if you want to master your chosen water-sport. Whether your interest is in surfing, windsurfing, canoeing, powerboats, dinghies or yachting, you are guaranteed expert tuition at whatever level you need. And you can book a weekend break or a holiday, or a course to suit your requirements. For further information ring 01646 636642.

Windsurfing
Age is no barrier to windsurfing, which attracts enthusiasts from 8 to 80. Some enjoy setting sail in light winds for a tranquil afternoon's cruise; others like to display their competitive streak by racing; and the most adventurous long for the exhilaration of strong winds and wave jumping in breaking surf.

Another big attraction of windsurfing is that it is easy to learn - provided you have the right equipment and tuition. One of Britain's top windsurfing and sailing venues is Dale. Its mile-wide bay promises superb sea sailing on flat water, with no strong tidal currents, and is ideal for beginners and experts alike. West Wales Windsurfing, Sailing and Canoeing, as described in the section on sailing, is based on Dale waterfront and is a specialist watersports centre approved by the Royal Yachting Association. The expert tuition available here caters for everyone, from absolute beginner to advanced windsurfer. All equipment is provided, including wetsuits and buoyancy aids, and every instructor holds a nationally recognised qualification.

As for recommending the best beaches, Broad Haven (St. Bride's Bay) and Newgale are ideal for more experienced windsurfers (except in particularly calm conditions), whereas beginners and intermediates will breeze along more easily at Tenby, Saundersfoot, Newport and Fishguard.

Haven Sports, Broad Haven: For more information ring 01437 781354.

Day Trips to Ireland

One of the great attractions of Pembrokeshire is its proximity to Ireland, and there are excellent daily car ferry services between the two.

In South Pembrokeshire, Irish Ferries operate to Rosslare from Pembroke Dock with their modern and comfortable ship *Isle of Innisfree*. You have the choice of afternoon or early morning sailing, and the crossing takes about 4 hours. In North Pembrokeshire, Stena Line also run to Rosslare, with departure from Fishguard. Their luxury ferry is the *Koningin Beatrix*, with a choice of restaurants and bars, plus lots of onboard entertainment for the crossing. Average sailing time to Rosslare from Fishguard is 31/2 hours. But if you're really in a hurry, you can opt for the high-speed SeaLynx. This service was introduced very successfully in 1994 and has reduced crossing times to just 99 minutes. In 1995 new improved port facilities were opened, including a comfortable new travel centre, duty-free shop, and greater emphasis on passenger comfort all round. Whatever your choice of port and vessel, you can cash in on a wide selection of duty-free goods. And if you make the crossing with your car during

Isle of Innisfree

early spring or autumn, money-saving discounts are available from both companies.

Stena Line: For people in a hurry, the 40 knot *Stena Lynx III* catamaran makes up to four return crossings daily in a time of just 99 minutes while the luxury *Koningen Beatrix* superferry is ideal for motorists wanting a rest and a relaxing break, especially those with children.

In the past year Stena Line has introduced a number of customer care service improvements on both the *Stena Lynx* and *Koningen Beatrix*. A Club Lounge facility offers preferential boarding for cars, a reserved seating area, dedicated waiter-service with complimentary refreshments, newspapers and magazines, queue-free shopping and if required, access to business facilities.

Both craft also operate a VJP (Very Junior Person) charter for infants, their parents and guardians. Cars travelling with babies are given special identification and convenient parking areas on deck, while on board VJPs have their own changing rooms and facilities for heating bottles and food.

And on board the *Koningen Beatrix*, Stena Line has set up the first ever supervised crèche at sea for 2 to 8 year olds, run by NNEB (National Nursery Examining Body) qualified staff. The ship also boasts a bigger soft play area, while during the school holidays, children's entertainers perform on board.

Throughout the year Stena Line presents regular entertainment cruises on board the *Koningen Beatrix* featuring tribute bands and stars of the 60s and 70s, while from spring to the autumn it has a great choice of day trips and coach tours to Ireland from south Wales. Trips include visits to Avoca, home to TV's Ballykissangel, the Irish National Heritage Park near Rosslare and the Waterford Crystal factory, as well as shopping trips to Wexford and Dublin.

And for longer stays Stena Line Holidays has a great choice of short breaks in hotels and self catering holidays for all the family, throughout Ireland.

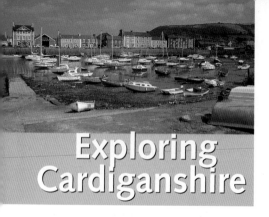

Exploring Cardiganshire

Just across the Teifi estuary from Poppit Sands and St. Dogmael's is the ancient county of Cardiganshire, or Ceredigion as it is now known in Welsh.

Like Pembrokeshire it is a county with a rich and varied landscape and a long and dramatic history. It is well known to countless holidaymakers as the home of such popular seaside resorts as New Quay, Aberaeron and Aberystwyth, and the spectacular coastline is marked by many fine beaches.The county and its impressive number of natural and man-made attractions are described in detail in The Premier Guide to Cardiganshire - a companion volume to this Pembrokeshire guide. Widely available throughout Cardiganshire or direct from Lily Publications, it follows the established and successful Premier Guide format, featuring a comprehensive beach guide, an A-Z listing and description of the towns and villages of Cardiganshire, and details of the county's many visitor attractions and sports and leisure facilities. In fact, The Premier Guide to Cardiganshire is an indispensable aid to visitors as it is the only guide dedicated entirely to this singularly beautiful county of West Wales.

For those who wish to stray over the border and explore Cardigan and its immediate area, here is a brief guide to some of the attractions to be found here.

Cardigan

Historic Cardigan, beautifully sited near the mouth of the River Teifi - hence the town's Welsh name of Aberteifi - is an important holiday centre, with some of Wales' most attractive coast and countryside right on the doorstep. To the east is the scenic Teifi Valley, and to the north is the spectacular Ceredigion coastline and its many beaches and resorts.

Cardigan received its first royal charter in 1199 from King John, and is the former county town of Cardiganshire. Still a thriving market town, it serves the local farming communities and is also a main shopping centre for the region. The Market Hall, built in 1859 and featuring impressive stone arches, holds a general market twice weekly and a livestock market once a week. The old character of the town is retained by its shops and narrow streets, and the visitor attractions include the Theatr Mwldan (housed in the same building as the Tourist Information Centre - both are open all year round), an indoor leisure centre, a golf club at nearby Gwbert, and a large annual arts festival, Gwyl Fawr Aberteifi. Crossing the Teifi below the castle is the striking multi-arched stone bridge. Sources disagree as to whether this is the original Norman bridge, strengthened and widened in later years, or whether it was

Mwnt

constructed in the 17th or even 18th century. The history of Cardigan Castle raises less argument. The ruins that now remain date from 1240, and it must have been in an earlier castle that the very first National Eisteddfod - 'advertised' for a whole year beforehand throughout Wales, England and Scotland - was hosted by Rhys ap Gruffudd in 1176. The National Eisteddfod is now the major cultural event in the Welsh calendar, as well as being Europe's largest peripatetic cultural festival. Cardigan Castle, like so many others, was destroyed by Cromwell; all that remains is now privately owned.

More recently, Cardigan was one of Wales' most prominent ports. As many as 300 ships were registered here, and shipbuilding thrived in the 19th century. The busy warehouses along the waterfront handled everything from exports of herring, corn, butter and slate to imports of limestone, salt, coal, timber for shipbuilding, and manufactured goods.

Human cargo was carried too: emigrant ships sailed from Cardigan to New York in the USA and New Brunswick in Canada.

This prosperous period for Cardigan was relatively short-lived, however. Inevitably, booming trade meant that ships were getting bigger all the time while the gradual silting of the estuary was making access to Cardigan more and more restricted. The final nail in the town's coffin as a commercial port was the coming of the railway in 1885 - but today, as a popular holiday destination, Cardigan is once again a busy centre of attention, boasting many attractions within easy reach. Several of these stand near the banks of the Teifi, such as St. Dogmael's Abbey, Poppit Sands, the Welsh Wildlife Centre, Cilgerran Castle and Cenarth Falls.

Theatr Mwldan: Cardigan A 200-seat theatre and cinema sited in historic buildings and hosting a varied programme of top-quality

drama, light entertainment, music, dance and film. The foyer houses the Tourist Information Centre, and there is also a bar and coffee shop. For performance details and bookings, ring the box office on 01239 621200.

Cardigan Swimming Pool & Leisure Complex: The superb indoor pool is complemented by first-class sports and games facilities, including a fitness suite. For more information ring 01239 613632 or 613056.

Teifi Leisure Centre, Cardigan: For more information ring 01239 621287.

Felinwynt Rainforest & Butterfly Centre: Step into this enlightening visitor attraction and you're immediately transported into a different world. A new tropical house was built in 1999 making the atmosphere of the rainforest startlingly real as you wander through the tropical and native plants, listening to the recorded sounds of the unique Peruvian Amazon.

New Quay

Beautiful, exotic butterflies fly freely around you. The humidity needed to sustain the plants and butterflies is provided by the waterfall, ponds and stream, which are inhabited by fish and amphibians. There is no admission charge to video or rainforest exhibition (based on the Tambopata Reserve in Peru). The Centre is 6 miles from Cardigan and 4 miles from Aberporth. Follow the signs on the A487 at Blaenannerch. For more information ring 01239 810882.

Cilgerran Castle: Cilgerran Castle is 3 miles south-east of Cardigan, in a dramatic position on a high bluff above the River Teifi. Seen from the deep wooded gorge below - as it was for centuries by the coracle fishermen - it presents a spectacular sight which inspired great landscape artists such as Turner and Richard Wilson.

Equally, the views which visitors can enjoy from its ruined towers are magnificent. The castle, small by comparison with Pembroke and the great Norman fortresses of North Wales, is mainly 13th century. Despite its apparently unassailable position, the castle changed hands many times between the 12th and 14th centuries. It was taken from the Normans by Lord Rhys in 1164; recaptured in 1204 by William Marshall; used as a base by Llewellyn the Great in 1215, when he summoned a Council of all Wales at Aberystwyth; taken again by the Normans in 1223, following which the present towers were built; and, after a period of decline and then refortification in the 14th century, was captured again for a brief period by the Welsh in 1405, during the uprising of Owain Glyndwr.

Welsh Wildlife Centre, Cilgerran: For further information about the Centre ring 01239 621600. For details of Wales Wildlife Trust, including membership, ring 01437 765462.

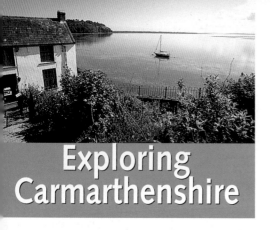

Exploring Carmarthenshire

Carmarthenshire is a very attractive holiday destination for visitors who appreciate history, culture and a green and beautiful environment. Covering an area of 1,000 square miles, the county is a veritable feast of delights and discovery - an intoxicating mix of glorious coast and countryside, offering a wealth of activities.

The county and its attractions are described in detail in The Premier Guide to Carmarthenshire - a companion volume to this Pembrokeshire guide. Widely available throughout West Wales or direct from Lily Publications, it follows the established and successful Premier Guide format, featuring a comprehensive beach guide, an A-Z listing and description of the towns and villages.

The 50 miles of stunning coastline embrace vast stretches of safe golden sands, such as the beaches of Cefn Sidan and Pendine, punctuated by the Taf and Towy estuaries, which so inspired Dylan Thomas. The Loughor estuary, a favourite haunt of migratory birds, is famous for its cockles - a delicacy to be found in the markets of Llanelli and Carmarthen.

The unspoilt and contrasting countryside of Carmarthenshire touches the edge of the Brecon Beacons National Park in the east, the Cambrian mountains in the north and the picturesque Teifi Valley to the west.

The county is also rich in bustling market towns, such as Newcastle Emlyn, Llandysul, Whitland, Llandeilo, Llandovery, Llanybydder and, of course, Carmarthen.

And the attractions and activities to be enjoyed in Carmarthenshire are many and varied - from castles, museums and art galleries to steam railways, country parks, fishing, golf, and the new National Botanic Gardens which opens this year. Not forgetting, of course, all that warm Welsh hospitality.

Carmarthen

At the heart of the county is the ancient township of Carmarthen. It stands on the River Towy, 8 miles inland - a position which inspired the Romans to make it their strategic regional capital. They also built an amphitheatre here, rediscovered in 1936 but first excavated in 1968. In legend, the town is the reputed birthplace of Merlin - wizard and counsellor to King Arthur.

Today, Carmarthen's quaint old narrow streets are full of Welsh character and tradition. There's also a first-class modern shopping centre with its many familiar high street names, and recently expanded with the opening of the Greyfriars shopping complex in the Autumn of 1998. This is complemented by Carmarthen's famous market, which, open six days a week attracts people from all over Wales. The colourful atmosphere is enriched by the banter and barter of the adjacent livestock mart - Wales' biggest. You're also likely to catch more than a smattering of

Carmarthen

172

HAMILTONS WINE BAR & BRASSERIE
QUEEN STREET, CARMARTHEN
TELEPHONE: (01267) 235631

A warm relaxing atmosphere to enjoy a pleasant lunch or evening meal.
A large selection of locally-caught seafood and char-grilled meats. Sunday Carvery and Salad Bar.

THE QUEENS
QUEEN STREET, CARMARTHEN
TELEPHONE: (01267) 231800

Typical Victorian Public House, selling a selection of Real Ales and home-cooked Bar Meals. Beer Garden.

173

Welsh, as it is still widely spoken here. It is believed that the oldest manuscript in the Welsh language - The Black Book of Carmarthen, now in the National Library of Wales in Aberystwyth - was written in the town.

For sport, there's the town's modern leisure centre, with its outstanding all-weather facilities. A few miles west is Derllys Court Golf Club, near Bancyfelin, which has an interesting 9-hole, pay as you play, par 35 course, set in a beautiful location amongst rolling countryside. There is a licensed bar and catering facilities. A warm welcome is extended to visitors, and club hire is available. For more information ring 01267 211575/211309

Another attraction virtually on Carmarthen's doorstep is the Gwili Railway at Bronwydd Arms (just off the A484)- one of Wales' last remaining standard-gauge steam railways. It takes you to a wooded riverside area deep in the valley, and there is also a picnic site. The railway opened in 1860 and eventually became the property of British Railways. After the remaining milk traffic was transferred to road, the line closed in 1973. The Gwili Railway Company was set up in 1975 and in 1978 a section of the line was reopened, run by volunteers. The railway currently runs over 1.6 miles from its southern terminus at Bronwydd Arms to a riverside station at Llwyfan Cerrig. An extension towards Cynwyl Elfed is progressing well.

Carmarthen Bay

South of Carmarthen, the River Towy emerges into Carmarthen Bay alongside the rivers Taf and Gwendraeth. This is an area of outstanding natural beauty, where scores of waders and seabirds take rich pickings from the broad expanse of mudflats formed by the three estuaries.

Here too you will discover the charming seaside villages of Ferryside and Llansteffan, at the mouth of the Towy. Just a short hop west to the Taf estuary takes you to Laugharne - a medieval township where the great poet

Laugharne Castle

and writer Dylan Thomas spent the latter years of his tragically short life. His home was the Boat House - his 'seashaken house on a breakneck of rocks', standing above the estuary - which is now a Heritage Centre dedicated to his memory.

From Laugharne, the road west cuts a picturesque route to Pendine Sands, where Sir Malcolm Campbell and others made several attempts on the world landspeed record, the most recent being in 1998. The fatal crash of Parry Thomas-Jones in 1927 ended Pendine's racing career, but the exciting new Museum of Speed recalls this village resort's days of fame and glory.

On the eastern side of Carmarthen Bay are the estuaries of the Gwendraeth and Loughor, and the superb seven-mile beach of Cefn Sidan Sands - one of the best beaches in Britain.

Quicksilver: Established in Laugharne for several years, Quicksilver produces an individual range of high quality but sensibly

175

priced silver jewellery in the workshop on the premises. Pieces are also made to order - to your own design if you wish - and you can choose a semi-precious stone from the attractive selection and have it set in a ring, bracelet, brooch or pendant, usually within an hour.

The emphasis at Quicksilver is on quality and choice, and every piece, whether it's a hallmarked chain or a bangle or ring is designed and made to last. For more information ring 01994 427700.

Whitland

Whitland stands on the River Taf inside the Carmarthenshire border, west of St. Clears. It rose in prominence as a market town in the 19th century, when the coming of the railway established it as an important junction. The town's most significant place in history goes back to the 10th century, when the great Welsh king Hywel Dda (Hywel the Good) called an assembly of wise men here to draw up a unified legal code for Wales, based on the ancient tribal laws and customs already in existence. The assembly took place at Ty Gwyn ar Daf (The White House on the Taf) - Hywel Dda's hunting lodge. It is thought that the house could have been the site chosen two centuries later for Whitland Abbey. The Hywel Dda Interpretive Gardens and Centre, in the centre of the town, now commemorate this great assembly.

Whitland Abbey was the first Cistercian monastery in Wales and gave rise to seven others, including Strata Florida. Founded in 1140, virtually nothing remains of the abbey today, its ruins standing to the north of Whitland.

Llanelli

Once the tinplate capital of the world, and arguably the home of Welsh rugby, Llanelli is a thriving town with an impressive pedestrianised shopping centre and bustling indoor and outdoor markets. Further development work to enhance these shopping facilitieshas now been completed.

Standing on the beautiful Loughor estuary, Llanelli has a pleasant beach and is close to many major attractions. These include Pembrey Country Park, magnificent Cefn Sidan Sands, the Pembrey Motorsports Centre and Kidwelly Castle. Places to visit in Llanelli itself include Parc Howard and Sandy Water Park.

For more detailed information on Llanelli and the surrounding region, see The Premier Guide to Swansea Bay & Gower, available from all good bookshops in the area or direct from Lily Publications.

Wildfowl & Wetlands Trust, Llanelli

Award winning WWT Llanelli is situated on the north shore of the Burry Inlet. It has stunning views over the estuary and Gower and with the opening of the new Millennium Discovery Centre and Millennium Wetland it is bigger and better than ever. The Discovery Centre, decked out as a house and with a talking tap in the bathroom, is crammed full of exciting activities for all ages. The

Millennium Wetland is an additional haven for both wildlife and visitors, including children who can explore Water Vole City and A Swan maze.

WWT Llanelli is open every day of the week, all year round. It is easily accessible from the M4 (Junction 47 or 48) and is situated just off the A484 (Llanelli to Swansea road), one mile east of Llanelli. Follow the brown duck signs. For further information phone 01554 741087.

Castles

Carmarthenshire boasts several outstanding examples of Norman castles. One of the best-preserved medieval fortresses in Wales is Kidwelly Castle, while the imposing ruins at Carreg Cennen and Llansteffan both enjoy elevated positions. And Laugharne Castle, where Dylan Thomas wrote Portrait of the Artist as a Young Dog, has been extensively refurbished by CADW (Welsh Historic Monuments) and is now open to visitors. Dinefwr Castle, near Llandeilo, is another sight not to be missed.

Cenarth

Cenarth is one of the most popular beauty spots in the whole of West Wales. It stands on the River Teifi and is a very pretty village, famous for its salmon-leap falls. It is also recognised as the traditional home of the Teifi coracle, and here you will find the National Coracle Centre, which despite its name is a private enterprise, though no less important or interesting for that. Unspoilt Cenarth is a designated conservation area, with many of its buildings listed. The fine old bridge is believed to be 18th century, and the flour mill which houses the Coracle Centre dates from the 1600's. Also of historical interest is St. Llawddog's church and its mysterious Sarsen Stone.

Coracle Centre & Mill, Cenarth: The strange, round fishing boat known as the coracle has been a familiar sight on the River Teifi for centuries. It is light, manoeuvrable and ideal in shallow water, though mastering the art of coracle fishing can take years of practice. Today there are still 12 pairs licensed to fish on the Teifi, but the best place to see coracles is here at the National Coracle Centre. The Centre houses over 20 different types of coracle, in varying shapes and sizes, from all over the world - India, Vietnam, Tibet, Iraq and North America - as well as 9 varieties of Welsh coracle and examples from England, Ireland and Scotland. In the workshop you can see how coracles are made. The Centre stands on the ground floor of a 17th-century flour mill, which is also open to visitors, and there are arts, crafts, souvenirs and gifts for sale.

The Old Smithy Craftshop & Heritage Centre, Cenarth: Within earshot of the falls, this fascinating attraction occupies a fully restored 18th-century blacksmith's forge which was last in operation in 1953. The Smithy's original equipment now forms part of an exhibition which also includes an interesting collection of Victorian rural antiques. Entry to the exhibition is free. The

Craftshop displays a wide selection of Celtic jewellery, Welsh woollens, wood carvings, local pottery, basketware, books and many more items. The old stone cottage adjoining the craftshop and heritage centre has played an important part in Cenarth's history. Once used as the vicarage, it also served as the village school and schoolmaster's residence until a new school was built in the 1860's. The Old Smithy Craftshop and Heritage Centre has a picnic area in the gardens, and parking is free. For more information ring 01239 710067

The Salmon Leap, Cenarth: For more information ring 01239 711242.

Newcastle Emlyn

The Bunch of Grapes The Bunch of Grapes is an attractive Public House built from stone from the castle and oak taken from Kent. It retains a traditional feel in both its ambience and tasteful decor with a wealth of oak beams. There is a covered interior garden with vines and cacti. The colourful garden at the rear is very sheltered and an excellent suntrap. The pub is featured in both the 'Good Pub Guide' and the 'Good Beer Guide' For further information phone 01239 711185

Teifi Valley Railway: For timetable and other enquiries ring 01559 371077.

Museum of the Welsh Woollen Industry : This fascinating museum is 5 miles east of

Nr Llandovery

Newcastle Emlyn, at Drefach Felindre - the very heart of the Welsh woollen industry at the beginning of the century, with more than 40 mills working in the area. The museum is situated alongside a mill which still works today, and is housed in the buildings of what used to be the Cambrian Mills - built in 1902 and one of the biggest producers in the Teifi Valley. The museum has facilities for the disabled and is situated off the A484 Carmarthen to Cardigan road. For more information ring 01559 370929.

Exploring Carmarthenshire

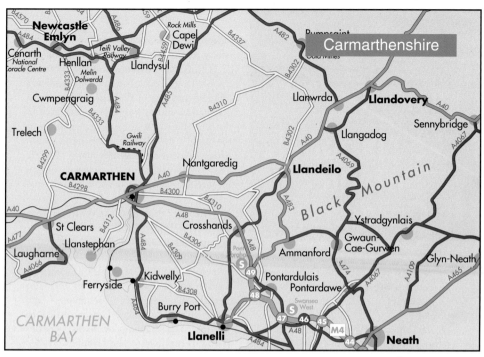

Carmarthenshire

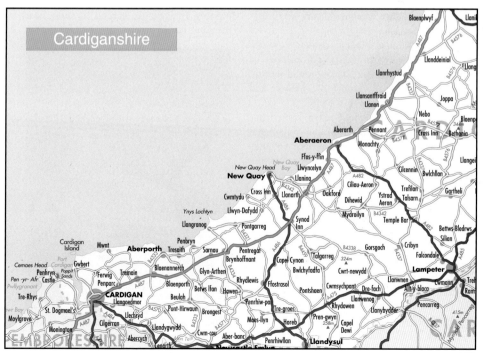

Cardiganshire

179

The National Botanic Gardens

The first national botanic garden to be created in the UK for more than 200 years is preparing to open to the public.

The Garden of Wales, set among the hills of the beautiful Towy Valley is south west Wales, will welcome visitors from May 2000 to an experience blending history with a 21st century outlook.

The National Botanic Garden of Wales, at Llanarthne in Carmarthenshire, is dedicated to science, education and leisure, with the broad study of plants and sustainable solutions at its heart.

The £43.3 million Garden, which has attracted £21.6 million from the Millennium Commission, is being created on a 568-acre regency estate. The Middleton Hall estate, developed by William Paxton in the late 1700s, has provided walled gardens, lakes and cascades for restoration.

The formal gardens with their centrepiece building, The Great Glasshouse, designed by Norman Foster and Partners, takes up about a third of this area. The rest of the land is made up of species-rich grassland and woodland which is being converted to a demonstration organic farm. In years to come visitors will be able to follow farm trails, picnic in the woods and explore a sustainable farm environment which, nevertheless, has to be self-financing.

The Great Glasshouse, at the centre of the Garden of Wales, is a futuristic landmark building and one of the largest single span glasshouses in the world. It is dedicated to the threatened Mediterranean climates of the world - the Mediterranean basin, south Africa, south west Australia, parts of Chile and California and its interior design includes a ravine, rock faces, waterwells and bridges.

The other features of the central Garden include the Hyder Water Discovery Centre, set on stilts above one of the seven lakes which form a necklace around the Garden; Principality House: The Lifelong Learning Centre where study groups can meet for workshops, lectures, seminars and conferences; The Walled Garden, dedicated to the understanding of plant genetics through the ages; The Double Walled Garden, an innovative design within an existing 18th century garden to show how mankind has used enclosed outdoor spaces

Working in the great glasshouse

The National Botanic Gardens

more than just a *Garden...*

Opening Spring 2000

Discover a garden of the world ...here in Wales

GARDD
FOTANEG GENEDLAETHOL
CYMRU

THE NATIONAL BOTANIC
GARDEN OF WALES

The National Botanic Garden of Wales
Middleton Hall, Llanarthne
Carmarthenshire SA32 8HG
☎ 01588 667134
www.gardenofwales.org.uk

181

across the world and across time. A Moghul garden will abut a Zen garden, a produce garden will sit next to a sensory space; the Broadwalk with its rill and fountains is a 220-metre-long herbaceous border providing a geological timewalk through the counties of Wales and linking the entrance Gatehouse with the Great Glasshouse and the visitor centre.

What might be termed the 'behind the scenes' operations of the Garden of Wales will also be on show to the public demonstrating the sustainable systems which allow the Garden to Function.

The Biomass Furnace uses chipped salvaged or coppiced wood to provide the heat for the site, the Living Machine is a sewage treatment works using plants to purify and filter the waste, and, all across the Garden, water is channelled and stored to be recycled for irrigation, the flushing of lavatories and the washing of machinery.

At the edges of the central Garden are the planting schemes that will help to establish the botanical and horticultural reputation of the Garden of Wales.

The Woods of the World will be informal semi-natural woodlands containing a wide range of species from areas of the world with similar climates to Wales. Among those represented will be south west China, parts of Chile, South Island New Zealand, Mexico, Highland Cameroon and the North West U.S.A. All the plants from the dominant tree species down through the shrub layer to the herbaceous plants that would normally be found in association with each other in these countries will be brought together and grown in as naturalistic manner as possible. Visitors will be able to walk through a Chinese woodland in Spring and see the blossom of the magnolias, rhododendrons and other woodland shrubs beneath a canopy of maples, handkerchief trees and witchhazel. All these plants will be grown from wild collected seed of known provenance

Inside the main glasshouse

enhancing the scientific conservation value of the collection.

A horticultural experiment is also underway to the east of the Great Glasshouse. The prairie project is the first to be tried on this scale in the UK. North American herbaceous perennials are being planted together in order to create a new concept of plant associations and an exciting display. This has not been tried in a wet climate before and there is no guarantee of success. It is possible that ten of the fifty species chosen for the site will not thrive but in this way the horticultural world and the visitor can follow the Garden's experimental journey and learn from it. The prairie planting, where herbaceous plants compete with one another in nutrient-poor soil, will constantly change, as will the information for people interested in the project.

More than thirty thousand people from all over the world have already visited The National Botanic Garden of Wales on preview visits to view the planning and construction of Wales' first and UK's last national botanic garden.

Pont Abraham Services
M4 Junction 49
Tel: 01792 884663 Fax: 01792 885365

Pont Abraham Services
M4 Junction 49
Tel: 01792 884663 Fax: 01792 885365

When you are travelling to and from West Wales why not stop for a break at RoadChef Pont Abraham.

We are conveniently situated just off junction 49 on the M4.

You'll find a full range of services along with a warm welcome and a friendly smile.

You can rest assured that when you come across the RoadChef sign you will be guaranteed quality service in very pleasant surroundings. So next time you're passing give yourself a break at Pont Abraham.

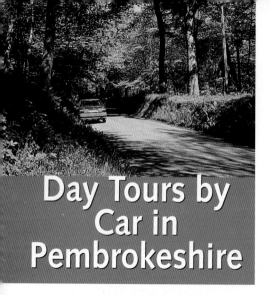

Day Tours by Car in Pembrokeshire

For those visitors who like to explore by car, these seven day drives will show you much of Pembrokeshire's varied landscape. The routes suggested cover the south, west, north and central regions of the county, and each tour is circular in that it takes you back to your starting point. Each is also intended as a leisurely drive, with plenty of points of interest along the way.

It is recommended that you use Ordnance Survey Landranger maps which cover Pembrokeshire - numbers 145 (north), 157 (north and west) and 158 (south) with these tours. These give detailed and valuable information to point you in the direction of attractions and places of interest you might otherwise miss. You should also bear in mind that filling stations in some of the remoter parts of Pembrokeshire are few and far between, so it is advisable to start your tour with plenty in the tank!

Tour1

Tenby-Carew-Llawhaden-Narberth-Amroth-Saundersfoot-Tenby

1. From Tenby take the B4318, signposted St. Florence. After Gumfreston note the magnificent views to your left across the Ritec Valley. After Manor House Leisure Park, turn left to the pretty village of St. Florence (church, flowers, Flemish-style chimney).

2. Leave village and return to the B4318, turning left. At Sageston turn left on the A477 towards Pembroke for three-quarters of a mile and then turn right on to the A4075 for Carew (castle, Celtic cross, mill, picnic area, 17th-century bridge). Cross the bridge and proceed up the hill, turning left on the minor road to Cresswell Quay (public house and attractive estuary scene, frequented by herons and kingfishers). Continue, following the signs to Lawrenny.

3. From Lawrenny (church, attractive village, estuary views from hillside car park) take the road to Lawrenny Quay (public house, yachting facilities, pleasant riverside walks and picnic site). Return to Lawrenny and turn left, following the road (Ordnance Survey Landranger map 158 will be useful) to Landshipping (a tiny hamlet with pleasant views over the estuary) and Landshipping Quay (a tranquil setting with riverside views, about half a mile further on). Return to Landshipping to continue.

4. From Landshipping follow the signs for Minwear (church and ancient woodland) and then on to Blackpool Mill (restored mill, cafe, gifts, riverside and woodland walks).

5. From the mill turn left, then left again on to the A4075, and down the hill to the A40 at Canaston Bridge. Go left towards Haverfordwest and turn right shortly after to Llawhaden (castle and beautiful parish church).

6. Turn left over the village bridge and follow the country lane to Pont-Shan (note lovely views of Llawhaden Church). Turn right at Pont-Shan on to the B4314 and follow this road to the town of Narberth (castle, church, information centre, market town).

7. Leave Narberth on the B4314 for Princes Gate, via Crinow. At Princes Gate, go straight on at the crossroads for Ludchurch (church) and follow the road for Longstone, again going straight on at the next crossroad for Colby Lodge (National Trust property and gardens).

8. From Colby Lodge proceed up the hill to the T-junction and turn right for Amroth (unspoilt coastal village with shops, pubs, restaurants, superb beach at low tide and seafront parking).

9. From Amroth proceed up the hill to the T-junction at Summerhill, turn left and follow the coast road, passing through Wiseman's Bridge and then on to the popular village resort of Saundersfoot (information centre, harbour,

superb beaches, tunnel walks to Wiseman's Bridge, shops and restaurants).

10.From Saundersfoot proceed out of the village up the hill to New Hedges and return to Tenby on the A478.

Tour 2

Tenby-Lydstep-Manorbier-Lamphey-Freshwater East-Stackpole-Pembroke-Carew-Tenby

1.Leave Tenby on the A4139, signposted Pembroke. As you approach Lydstep village (shortly after the entrance to Lydstep Haven holiday park), note the pull-in on the left-hand side of the road giving superb views of Caldey Island and the cliffs towards Giltar Point.

2.After passing through Lydstep village, turn left to Manorbier (B4585) at the crossroads. For a detour to one of the best beaches in Pembrokeshire, follow the signs to Skrinkle Haven (i.e. a left turn through Skrinkle estate, towards the Royal Artillery range.) There is good parking for the beach and coast path, with excellent coastal views. Retrace your steps back to the B4585 and turn left to Manorbier village and car park (Norman castle and church, village shops, pub, cafe and beach).

3.Leave Manorbier on the B4585 signposted Pembroke and rejoin the A4139. Proceed through Jameston and Hodgeston and on to Lamphey (medieval Bishop's Palace).

4.From Lamphey take the B4584 to Freshwater East (beach, sand dunes, coast path, views), turning right down the steep winding hill in the village to the beach and car park.

5.Cross the small narrow bridge by the beach and follow the road through East Trewent for about 2 miles. Turn left (no through road) for Stackpole Quay (small harbour, large car park, and coast path to Barafundle beach - the only access - and to Stackpole Head and beyond, with stunning views).

6.Return to the T-junction and turn left to the village of Stackpole, following the road through National Trust woodland to the B4319. Turn right for Pembroke (magnificent medieval castle, National Park and Tourist Information centres, shops, restaurants, town walks,

millpond walk, plenty of car parking).

7.Leave Pembroke along Main Street, turning left at the A4075, signposted St. Clears. At the major junction with the A477, turn right. After about 2 miles turn left (rejoining the A4075) for Carew (medieval castle, Celtic cross, tidal mill, walks, pub, cafe and riverside picnic area). Return to the A477 and turn left. Immediately after Sageston turn right on to the B4318, signposted Tenby.

Tour 3

Pembroke-Bosherston-St. Govan's*-Stack Rocks*-Castlemartin-Freshwater West-Angle-Pembroke

(*Please note that the roads to St. Govan's and Stack Rocks are closed at certain times. Dates of closure are published in advance in the local press.)

1.From Pembroke take the B4319 (south of the town) for Bosherston. After about 3 miles note St. Petrox Church on your right. Continue, turning left at the signpost for Bosherston (church, lakes, lily ponds, fishing, superb walks, wildlife, access to Broadhaven beach, pub and cafe). There is a large National Trust car park close to the church and lily ponds.

2.Continue through Bosherston, turning left for Broad Haven (large clifftop car park, outstanding views, superb beach).

3.Re-trace the road back to Bosherston, turning left in the village for St Govan's Head (large car park, remarkable chapel in the cliffs, coast path, spectacular views, dramatic coastal features such as Huntsman's Leap, excellent walks towards Stackpole Head to the east and Stack Rocks and the Green Bridge of Wales to the west).

4.Retrace your steps through Bosherston to the B4319 and turn left for Castlemartin. After you pass Merrion Camp, where two tanks are on display at the entrance, turn left for Stack Rocks. The road passes medieval Flimston Chapel (restored) and leads to a large clifftop car park. Stack Rocks (two vertical columns, home to thousands of breeding seabirds in early summer) stand just offshore a few hundred yards to your left, and a short distance to your right is a viewing platform for the Green Bridge of Wales (a spectacular limestone arch).

185

5.Return to the B4319 and turn left for Castlemartin, where an 18th-century circular stone cattle pound is now a traffic roundabout. Fork left for Freshwater West (a long, wide beach backed by rolling sand dunes, with a restored beach hut once used for drying seaweed to make laverbread). As you descend the hill to the car park there is a panoramic view of the bay.

6.Continue along the coast road, which gives more superb views as it climbs again towards a T-junction. Turn left here (B4320) for Angle, passing the huge Texaco refinery and views across the estuary towards Milford Haven and the busy shipping lanes.

7.In the old fishing village of Angle, which lies between East Angle Bay and West Angle Bay, interesting sights include the church and the remains of the medieval Tower House. West Angle Bay (beach, cafe, easy parking, views of Thorn Island and the Haven, outstanding coastal walks in either direction) and East Angle Bay (pub, lifeboat station, yacht moorings, outstanding views and walks) are well worth seeing. Return to Pembroke on the B4320 (about a 10-mile drive) via Hundleton.

Tour 4

Haverfordwest-Milford Haven-Dale-Marloes-Little Haven-Broad Haven-Nolton Haven-Newgale-Haverfordwest

1.Leave Haverfordwest on the A4076, passing through Johnston.

2.Milford Haven offers easy parking at both the Rath and the new marina. Attractions at the latter include a museum, Kaleidoscope Discovery Centre, adventure playground, crafts gallery, choice of eating places, 9-hole golf course, boat trips, pleasant walks and views along the Haven waterway, and much more.

3.From Milford Haven, follow the road signposted Herbrandston and Dale, eventually joining the B4327 from Haverfordwest about two and a half miles from Dale (village, beach, watersports, views of the Haven).

4.From the village proceed to St. Ann's Head (lighthouse, outstanding views of the Atlantic and the entrance to the Haven waterway), leaving your car in the car park to your right just before the lighthouse and the

headland.

5.Retrace your journey to Dale. From here you can take a detour to West Dale Beach (well worth the time) by turning left by the church and leaving your car at the end of the road.

6.From Dale take the B4327 for about one and a half miles and turn left to Marloes. Before reaching the village go left for Marloes Sands (one of Pembrokeshire's most beautiful beaches), parking your car at the end of the road.

7.Return to Marloes (clock tower) and follow the signs for Martin's Haven. The coast road culminates in a National Trust car park, and a walk from Martin's Haven to the headland will give you outstanding views of Skomer, Skokholm and St. Bride's Bay. (Boat trips run to Skomer from Martin's Haven, as described in the chapter on Pembrokeshire's islands.).

8.Return to Marloes and follow the signs for Dale, turning left at the T-junction. After about a quarter of a mile turn left for St. Bride's (beach, views, walks, limited parking).

9.Your next port of call is the small, pretty seaside village of Little Haven (parking, beach, views, walks, pottery, pubs and shops), which is accessible via various country lanes that take you through Talbenny.

10.From Little Haven follow the road out to Broad Haven (easy parking, long beach, water-sports, outstanding views and walks, interesting rock formations, shops and other facilities).

11.From Broad Haven take the coast road north for Nolton Haven. After passing through Haroldston West turn left for Druidston Haven (beach, views) and continue to Nolton Haven (beach, walks, views). The narrow coast road takes you on to Newgale (long beach, water-sports, views towards nearby St. David's). From Newgale take the A487 to Haverfordwest, returning via Roch (castle) and Simpson Cross.

Tour 5

Haverfordwest-Clarbeston Road-Llysyfran-Maenclochog-Rosebush-Gwaun Valley-Dinas Cross-Fishguard-Strumble Head-Mathry-Letterston-Treffgarne Gorge-Haverfordwest

1.Leave Haverfordwest on the Withybush and Crundale road (B4329) and at Crundale turn right on to the minor road signposted Clarbeston Road and Llysyfran.

2.Carefully follow the signs from here for Llysyfran Country Park (reservoir, fishing, sailing, walks, wildlife, activities, visitor centre, restaurant, picnic sites and more).

3.From the country park rejoin the road to nearby Gwastad. A short detour to New Moat (church) is well worthwhile. Return to the Gwastad road and go on to the pretty village of Maenclochog (church).

4.Follow the B4313 to Rosebush (views, walks, slate quarries, restaurant), and continue to the crossroads at New Inn. Turn right here (B4329) and climb to one of the highest points of the Preseli Hills, where a car park on your right (and a short walk up to Cerrig Lladron) give superb views. Return to the crossroads at New Inn, turning right on to the B4313 for Fishguard.

5.Continue along the B4313 for about 5 miles and turn left down the hill for Pontfaen (picturesque Gwaun Valley). After the village bridge go straight on at the crossroads and up the very steep hill for Dinas Cross.

6.This moorland road gives outstanding views across Newport Bay before descending to Dinas Cross.At the T-junction turn right on to the A487 and turn immediately left for Pwllgwaelod (beach, views, cafe).

7.Return to the A487, turn left and then go left again for Cwm-yr-Eglwys (beach, ruined church, views) along the narrow road. Return to the A487 and turn right for Fishguard.

8.After about 2 miles, turn left for Llanychaer. This road is very narrow and steep in places. After passing over the bridge in the village, rejoin the B4313, turning right for Fishguard (busy ferry port with shops, cafes, restaurants, information centres). Lower Fishguard, where the Gwaun runs into the sea, is very picturesque and a popular film location.

9.Take the road from Fishguard to Goodwick. At the bottom of the hill is a large car park with good views of the bay and the daily ferries operating to Rosslare in Ireland.

10.At the roundabout, by the Stena Line terminal, proceed up the hill and follow the signs for Strumble Head (car park, lighthouse, views, walks), turning right for the headland after about 2 miles.

11.Retracing your steps along the narrow headland road, turn right to Garn Fawr. At the top of the hill is a car park on your right, and the footpath gives outstanding views across the county and towards Strumble Head.

12.Follow the coast road towards Mathry, taking a detour to Melin Tregwynt Mill.

13.On reaching the A487, turn right up the hill to the village of Mathry (unusual parish church, stunning views, ancient burial site nearby).

14.Return to the A487 and take the B4313 to Letterston. Turn right at the crossroads in the village on to the A40 and head back to Haverfordwest via Treffgarne Gorge (Nant-y-Coy Mill, striking rock formations and spectacular views).

Tour 6

Haverfordwest-Newgale-Solva-Middle Mill-St.David's-Abereiddy-Porthgain-Abercastle-Trevine-Haverfordwest

1.Leave Haverfordwest on the A487 for St. David's, passing through Simpson Cross and Roch (castle). As you approach Newgale there are superb views over St. Bride's Bay.

2.From Newgale continue to Solva (beautiful natural harbour, pretty village, shops, excellent walks). Don't miss the short detour from Solva to picturesque Middle Mill (working woollen mill, picnic site).

3.Return to Solva and the coast road (A487) takes you on to the tiny city of St. David's (cathedral, Bishop's Palace, walks, shops, restaurants, art galleries, activities, information centre).

4.From the centre of St. David's take the minor road to Porth Clais (picturesque little harbour) and on to St. Justinian (lifeboat station, views across the sound to Ramsey Island).

5.Return to St. David's and follow the signs for Fishguard (A487) for a short distance, forking left on to the B4583 to Whitesands Bay (outstanding European Blue Flag beach, walks, views). Return towards the A487 but just before reaching it turn left for Abereiddy (beach, walks, Blue Lagoon, access to the neighbouring beach of Traeth Llyfn).

6.Follow the signs from Abereiddy along the coast to Llanrhian (church) and turn left for Porthgain (picturesque harbour, walks).

7.Returning to Llanrhian, turn left for Trevine (youth hostel, partly restored mill, handweaving centre and craft shop) and follow the signs for Abercastle (harbour, coastal walks, Carreg Sampson burial chamber).

8.Follow the road out of Abercastle for the village of Mathry (unusual church, views). Go down the hill out of the village and take the B4331 to Letterston, where you turn right on to the A40.

9.Return to Haverfordwest via Treffgarne Gorge (Nant-y-Coy Mill, striking rock formations and spectacular views).

Tour 7

Fishguard-Dinas-Cross-Newport-Nevern-Moylegrove-Poppit-Sands-St Dogmael's-Cardigan-Gwbert-Mwnt-Llechryd-Cilgerran-Blaenffos-Preseli Hills-Rosebush-Gwaun Valley-Fishguard

1.Leave Fishguard on the A487, signposted Cardigan, passing through Lower Fishguard en-route to Dinas Cross (for detours to Cwm-yr-Eglwys and Pwllgwaelod, see Tour 5). Continue along the A487 to Newport (town, beaches, castle, views).

2.From Newport the next stop is Nevern, just off the A487, but before this two detours are recommended. The first is to one of Britain's best prehistoric burial chambers - Pentre Ifan (OS.101370). To find it, turn right off the A487 before the Nevern turn-off and follow the narrow country lanes to the top of the hill. The second detour is to Castell Henllys (OS.118391), a reconstructed Iron Age fort managed by the National Park Authority. After either or both detours, return to the A487 and head back towards Newport, turning right for the village of Nevern (church, Celtic cross, pilgrims' cross).

3.From Nevern proceed up the hill on the B4582 and take the third left-hand turn, signposted Moylegrove (attractive coastal village dating back to Norman times). Near the bottom of the hill in the village turn left along the narrow road to Ceibwr Bay (pebble beach, picnic sites, panoramic views, excellent walks along the coast path in both directions).

4.Retrace your route to Moylegrove, turning left in the village to follow the narrow country lanes to Poppit Sands (large sandy beach, car park, cafe, lifeboat station, views of the Teifi estuary, interesting seabirds and waders, outstanding countryside and walks).

5.From Poppit Sands the B4586 follows the estuary to St. Dogmael's (attractive hillside village, ruins of a 12th-century Benedictine abbey, parish church containing the Sagranus Stone).

6.The B4586 takes you through the village to the A487, where you turn left and cross the bridge to Cardigan (historic market town, shops, twice-weekly market, theatre, information centre, leisure centre, scant castle ruins).

7.From the town centre proceed along the northern bank of the River Teifi to Gwbert (golf club, views across the estuary to Poppit Sands). From Gwbert take the country lanes to Mwnt (superb secluded beach, fishing, chapel, outstanding views and walks) via Ferwig.

8.Follow the signs to Cardigan, bypassing Ferwig and Gwbert, and from the town centre take the A484 to Llechryd. Turn right in the village for Cilgerran (castle, village, views, coracles on the Teifi, Welsh Wildlife Centre).

9.From Cilgerran head south to Rhos-Hill, where you join the A478 and go left for the village of Crymych. Just after leaving the village, turn right for Mynachlogddu. This country road takes you through the heart of the Preseli Hills.

10.At Mynachlogddu proceed south for about 1 mile to view the standing stones at Gors Fawr (OS.135294). Return towards the village and turn left along a winding country lane for Rosebush (views, walks, slate quarries, restaurant), turning right on to the B4313 to reach the village.

11.Continue to the crossroads at New Inn and go straight on for Fishguard. This road takes you alongside the beautiful Gwaun Valley, and detours to see the villages of Pontfaen and Llanychaer (both signposted) are recommended.

ACKNOWLEDGEMENTS

Thanks are due to all those people who have helped in the compilation and production of this revised edition. In particular the author is indebted to Llywela Harris (St. David's Cathedral Festival), Sue Dewley (Wales Tourist Board), Peter Bounds, David Lemon, Chris Warren, Linda Cowsill, Pat and Geoff Somner, Clare and Neil Price, Andrew Lowe and the staff of Haven Colourprint.

191

We hope you have enjoyed reading and using this book.There are now eight other titles in the growing *Premier Guide* series, six of which focus on different areas of Wales. The continued success and popularity of these guides means that more are in the pipeline. Our current titles (listed on the back cover of this guide) are available from branches of WH Smith and other leading bookshops and retailers, or direct from:

Lily Publications, PO Box 9, Narberth, Pembrokeshire, SA68 0YT

Tel: (01834) 891461 Fax: (01834) 891463